Peter M. Rookey, O.S.M.

SHEPHERD OF SOULS
Father Anthony M. Pucci, O.S.M.
The Little Pastor of Viareggio

Servite Priest - Pastor - Saint

ORDER OF FRIAR SERVANTS OF MARY
USA PROVINCE
CHICAG0, ILLINOIS
2002

SHEPHERD OF SOULS
Father Anthony M. Pucci, O.S.M.

By: Peter M. Rookey, O.S.M.

ISBN# 1-891280-44-9

Publisher:
CMJ Marian Publishers
Soul Assurance Prayer Plan
Post Office Box 661
Oak Lawn, Illinois 60454
www.cmjbooks.com
jwby@aol.com

Manufactured in the United States of America

Graphic Design:
Contact Publisher for information

Table of Contents

THE MIRACLE PRAYER

Lord Jesus, I come before you, just as I am. I am sorry for my sins, I repent of my sins, please forgive me. In your name, I forgive all others for what they have done against me. I renounce Satan, the evil spirits and all their works. I give you my entire self, Lord Jesus, now and forever. I invite you into my life, Jesus. I accept you as my Lord, God and Saviour. Heal me, change me, strengthen me in body, soul and spirit.

Come Lord Jesus, cover me with your precious blood, and fill me with your **Holy Spirit, I Love You Lord Jesus. I Praise You Jesus.** I thank you Jesus. I shall follow you every day of my life. Amen.

Mary my mother, Queen of Peace, St. Peregrine, the cancer saint, all you Angels and Saints, please help me. Amen.

© 1993 Servite Fathers, O.S.M.

Say this prayer faithfully, no matter how you feel, when you come to the point where you sincerely mean each word, with all your heart, something good spiritually will happen to you. You will experience Jesus, and HE will change your whole life in a very special way. You will see.

Imprimatur † Francisco Maria Aguilera Gonzalez, Auxiliary Bishop of Mexico, September 8, 1992

AVE MARIA!
SHEPHERD OF SOULS
INTRODUCTION TO THE THIRD PRINTING

Maria Valtorta, S.O.S.M. was a Secular Servant of Mary, or Servite, like St. Anthony Mary Pucci. She lived her "Victim Soul" life in Viareggio, Italy, where St. Anthony was pastor for forty-five years. There she wrote *Poem Of The Man-God*. She took the vows, poverty, chastity and obedience. Our Lord revealed to Maria that she would identify with Him as a "Victim Soul" in 1931.

Jesus died in 33 A.D. In 1233 Our Lady chose seven lay merchants of Florence, Italy as Her first special Servants. In 1933, Maria Valtorta began to experience great sufferings confining her to her home in Viareggio - In her suffering she imitated Jesus and His mother, the Patroness of Servites.

Between 1944 - 1947, Our Lord seemed to favor her with visions of His life and Mother Mary's life. He commanded Maria to write everything carefully. St. John's Gospel ends: "Now there are many other things that Jesus did."*[1] Jesus allegedly "dictated" to Maria many of these "other things" which the Evangelists' four brief accounts omit. In April, 1947, the 5000 page *Poem Of The Man God* was ready.

Shortly thereafter, my dear saintly brother Servite, Fr. Conrad Mary Berti, Professor at Marianum University,

---

[1] John 21:25

1

Rome[2]** submitted the first copy to Pope Pius XII.

On February 26, 1948, Pope Pius XII received three Servites in private audience: Fr. Conrad Mary Berti, Fr. Andrew Mary Cecchin, Prior at Marianum and Fr. Romuald Mary Migliorini,[3] former Vicar Apostolic of Swaziland, Africa.

The Pope told them: "Publish this work as it is. There is no need to give an opinion about its origin, whether it is extraordinary or not. Who reads it will understand. One hears of many visions and revelations. I will not say they are authentic; but there are some of which it could be said they are authentic."

Maria wrote almost 15,000 pages including the Poem. She finished her autobiography and began the "dictations" of the *Poem Of The Man-God* on Good Friday, 1943, and continued during WWII until 1953, the year I took up

---

[2] See - Inside the Vatican, April 1996

[3] Spiritual Director of Maria to whom she addresses her autobiography. I knew all three priests personally as Assistant General of the Servites six years in Rome.In fact, Maria Valtorta writes in her note-book pg.201, July 6,1943: "Thank you Fr. Migliorini for having followed Jesus' inspiration and given me the life of the Cure' of Ars to read again. It pleases me very much because he is a victim soul."

residence in Rome at San Marcello al Corso. She worked ill in bed, a Victim Soul for 28 years. Maria died October 12[4], 1961. Two years later on October 12th, the Servites were allowed to transfer her remains from Viareggio to the Servite Basilica of the Annunciation, Florence. She is venerated to this day as one of the greatest mystics of all time.

See *Victim Souls*, Edited by In Wahreit Und Treve Posfach 279 CH-8401 Winterthur, Switzerland.

Popes, cardinals, bishops, clergy, scripture scholars and people the world over have praised her works. Many have had their lives changed through these inspired writings which illuminate the word of God. I, myself, and many, many priests and Christian leaders use them to evangelize.

It seems our Lord used St. Anthony Mary Pucci to set the stage for Maria Valtorta's dramatic life and mystique. Like the Cure' of Ars, St. Anthony spiritually renewed Viareggio. The Lord crowned his efforts using Maria Valtorta.

---

[4] Fr. Rookey's birthday (October 12).

Some years before, a simple pastor, St. John Mary Vianney, renewed the community of Ars, France. How the Lord uses the humble, like Mary, "to do great things!" Holy is His Name.

Chroniclers tell of the Cure' of Ars, St. John Mary Vianney and his struggle with studies. A panel of professors was giving his final examinations before priestly ordination. St. John was not responding too well. In desperation the lead professor threw up his hands "What would the Lord do with a jackass like this?"

The Cure' of Ars answered: "If the Lord through Samson could slay a thousand Philistines with just the jawbone of an ass, what could the Lord do with a whole jackass!"

Lord, use this writer as your donkey to carry you in triumph into the heavenly Jerusalem!

Peter Mary Rookey, O.S.M.
October 12, 1996
Our Lady of Sorrows Servite Basilica
3121 West Jackson Blvd.
Chicago, Illinois 60612
USA

August 2, 1985

Dear Peter,

I Have just finished reading your <u>Shepherd of Souls</u>. Congratulations for a job well done!

The format is exceedingly attractive, it is easy to read, interesting, and uplifting. Not only is it a significant contribution to Servite history, but an excellent source of spiritual reading as well.

You deserve the gratitude of all Servites for your doubtlessly considerable efforts in bringing this publication to the light of day. May it enjoy the widespread dissemination and acclaim it so widely deserves.

Fraternally,

John M. Huels, O.S.M.

SHEPHERD OF SOULS

BY
FATHER PETER MARY ROOKEY O.S.M.

This book is the work of many hours, searching, painstaking examination of documents and people. It should be a guide for all people, not only Servites.

Can we be like St. Anthony Mary Pucci who lived the words given to St. Peter, "Feed My Sheep, Feed My Lambs."

St. Anthony Mary Pucci was not only a servant of Mary, but a servant of all our brothers and sisters, he loved so much, can we love as much?

Joseph D. Molloy S.O.S.M.

Shepard of Souls

PREFACE

I would like to thank my religious superiors, who placed me in Rome, Italy at the time when Father Anthony Mary Pucci's cause was being considered. This drew me to Viareggio where I researched much of this book.

Then I wish to express my gratitude to Bernard Verwiel, without whose encouragement and criticism, the manuscript would not have left its shelf. My thanks also to his student, Terry Sullivan, for her invaluable assistance in reading the manuscript for continuity and clarity

Special thanks to Rev. Conrad M. Borntrager, 0. S. M., Historian and Archivist of the Servite Eastern Province for evaluating the manuscript for historical accuracy.

My gratitude goes also to Rev. Lawrence M. Choate, 0. S. M., Professor at the Marianum Faculty in Rome, for his assistance with this literary endeavor.

A special "Thank you" to Mildred Morrison, former secretary to the Provincial of Our Lady of Sorrows Province of Servites, for editing the manuscript and typing same.

I am grateful to Elizabeth Bellerive for permitting me to use her original oil painting of "A Servite Monk" to illustrate my book.

I especially thank Richard Locher, Pulitzer Prize Winner of the Chicago Tribune for his original sketch of Saint Anthony Pucci created for this biography.

Gratitude also to Mr. James Gilboy, Marian Publishers, who personally initiated this third revamped edition of Shepherd of Souls*.*

Finally I wish to express my gratitude to Our Lady of Sorrows for giving me the impetus to write about one of the priests of the Order dedicated to her, Father Anthony Pucci, O.S.M., the Little Pastor of Viareggio.

Peter M. Rookey, O.S.M.

Our Lady of Sorrows Monastery

Chicago, Illinois

12 February 1985

INTRODUCTION

The Second Vatican Council Fathers, led by Blessed Pope John XXIII who convoked the Council, keynoted the pastoral life. The Holy Father who wanted to be known as a pastor of his flock, emphasized this by closing the first session of Vatican II with the canonization of a model pastor; Anthony Mary Pucci of the Order of Servants of Mary (Servites).

Father Anthony, modern parish priest, embodied the Council's ideals of a pastor. He was a humble, dedicated leader whose twofold purpose was to serve his Lord and to lead his flock to God.

On November 16, 1961, Pope John XXIII, expounding the virtues of a true pastor, remarked: "He must be above all a man of prayer, of mortification, and of sincere humility." This personal sanctity is "the secret of every successful apostolate" (Osservatore Romano, Nov. 16, 1961). As you follow the life of St. Anthony, Pastor of Viareggio, note that he lived these three virtues. In addition, he displayed organizational acumen in a time when parish organizations were something of a novelty.

May the priestliness and saintliness of Father Anthony Pucci be a vanguard for our parish priests now in the 2000 millenium just as they were for the Second Vatican Council Fathers when the Little Pastor of Viareggio was proclaimed a Saint.

I.   JOURNEY TO VIAREGGIO

While I was Assistant to Father General in June of 1962, I felt compelled to obtain permission to travel from Rome to Viareggio to uncover for posterity some of the history of the boy Eustace Pucci who became a priest of the Order of Servants of Mary. Father General gave the willing nod and I left San Marcello for the journey.

Where is Viareggio? Take out your map of Europe. Find Italy's boot and run your finger up the Mediterranean side. There you will find the little fishing and resort city of Viareggio just above Pisa. Roughly translated "Kingsway," Viareggio has always been a popular resort on the Italian Riviera. One of the monuments there today is that to Percy Bysshe Shelley, famous poet, who drowned at Viareggio in 1822. According to the *Encyclopedia Americana,* population now is 65,000. In the last century only 3,000 to 4,000 lived there. In our century, former American Ambassador to Italy, Clare Booth Luce, often vacationed at Viareggio.

From Rome I took the train to Florence to visit some of the places so dear to Father Anthony Pucci. I visited Monte Senario, cradle of the religious Order of Servants of Mary, the scene of his early Servite training; also, the Monastery of the Annunziata down in the city, attached to the Basilica. Here, before the miraculous image of the Annunciation, the Medici prayed. Later, at this same spot, St. Aloysius Gonzaga made his vow of chastity. Here, also, Pope John XXIII celebrated one of his first Masses as a newly-ordained priest. And here Eustace Pucci resided for many years as a student and as a novice.

From Florence I went to Pisa to see Father Sostene Benedetti, O.S.M., retired pastor of the Servite church there, who knew more than any man then living about Father Anthony Pucci. Much of what I write about Anthony is owed to Father Benedetti and his sources.

"So glad that you are writing on *Il Curatino* (the Little Pastor)," said Father Benedetti. We sat down in his room. It was filled with hundreds of papers and souvenirs of our Saint Anthony Pucci. You might say that Father Benedetti loved Anthony Pucci as a brother. It was he who interested the Father General and the authorities in the Diocese of Pistoia in the cause of St. Anthony. That was back in the teens of this century. He got right down to business.

"You know," he continued, "I have checked the marriage book, for the marriage of Augustine Pucci and Mary Olive Macchi. They're his father and mother. Practically all the authors on St. Anthony have the date for the marriage wrong. They married in Cavarsano, Church of St. Peter, Apostle, September 27,1815.

"The first child arrived August 21,1816. They named her Maria. [5] They called all the girls Maria...Maria Merope... then on April 16, 1819, Eustace (St. Anthony) first saw light of day at nine o'clock in the morning. After dinner the

---

[5] Maria Monica (II) named for the child that died was born February 11, 1832. She died just before World War I, in 1913. Maria Elena (adopted), born May 3, 1834, probably called Helen because May 3rd is the feast of the Finding of the Holy cross in Jerusalem by Constantine's mother, St. Helen. Maria "Helen" died in 1851.

family traveled several miles, brought him to Vernio. (Poggiole was so small the church had no baptismal font). Only five hours after she gave birth to her saintly son, Mary Olive Pucci and her husband had him already regenerated in the baptismal font... What great faith they had! [6]

"I was a small child in Viareggio when Father Antonio Maria Pucci, the Parish Priest of Viareggio, died. Father Joachim Ducceschi was the first one to collect information and facts about him.

"It was all a work of God.

"We received permission to take Father Pucci's remains from the cemetery in Viareggio to the parish church of St. Andrew. That was in 1920... I received 500 lire from my brother to print my short biography of the Saint *(An Apostle of Charity,* Viareggio, 1920).

"Queen Helen, wife of Victor Emmanuel III also gave me 1000 lire. That was all I had to begin with. So you may say the cause began with nothing.

---

[6] Other children in the Augustine Pucci - Mary Olive Macchi family documented by

Father Benedetti that he told me about on this occasion:

Luigi Xanobi, born June 20, 1821; died ten years later on July 15, 1831

Euphemia Demetria, born October 22, 1823.

Twins: Fausto and Maria Faustina, born June 9, 1826. Fausto died December 18, 1842 when he was only 17 years old.

Maria Faustina died in 1852.

Maria Monica, born June 27, 1829; died an infant.

"I also interested the Postulator General of our Servite saints in Rome. The Father General, (later Cardinal) Lepicier said that" 'Father Anthony Pucci had the makings of a saint`. I went ahead.

"The parishioners in Viareggio formed a Holy Communion society to further the cause. The group also gave of their modest means."

"Interested people from America sent donations... The process for the cause of Father Anthony began in Lucca. Viareggio is in the Diocese of Lucca. Two years later it was taken up in Rome.

"During these anxious years 1922-23, I prayed so hard... One night I heard a voice, very clearly: 'You will not die before Father Anthony is raised to the altars.'

"If Father Anthony becomes canonized it will be nothing short of a miracle; the brethren of his household were all against him."

Suddenly dear old Father Benedetti switched the conversation. He began talking about a certain Father Poletti. This priest worked with Father Pucci as assistant pastor to him. The members of the board for the process in Lucca asked Father Poletti to testify.

"'Me, testify? retorted Poletti. 'I know too much. I wouldn't want to stand in the way of his becoming canonized! Father Benedetti asked him. He refused. He asked him again and again. Finally he gave in. After outlining many human faults and failings in Father Pucci's person he concluded: 'However; I remarked *no moral fault* in Father Pucci.'

This star witness who had lived intimately with the saint for many years could not have given a finer testimonial.

* * *

The bus from Pisa to Viareggio takes you the fourteen miles along the majestic shoreline that is Mediterranean Italy. The language - staccato music of modernized Latin-Italian - is familiar. Our bus stops in the main piazza. From there I wend my way to the Church and Servite Priory of Sant'Andrea, on the Via Sant'Andrea, 31, just a few blocks from the sea.

The church is sturdy romanesque, with massive marble columns supporting the structure on either side, leading down the nave to the main altar and choir. To the left is the altar to Anthony Pucci. His body is there in a glass vault for all the world to see. I breathed a prayer for all those who are devoted to this saint, each one. To the right of the main altar is the altar of Our Lady of Sorrows, surmounted by the statue of Our Lady which Father Anthony commissioned. Only the tower is different now. Near Anthony's altar is an inscription noting that it was destroyed during World War II in 1944 and reconstructed to the side of the church instead of at the apse.

Father Thomas Banci, the Prior, received me warmly, as did the other eight Servites in the community. Father Forconi, pastor and successor to Anthony Pucci, the 'Little Pastor of Viareggio', rose to bid me welcome. It was Pentecost Tuesday, and the Mass we celebrated for this day was the Mass of the Good Shepherd, which seemed to be providentially significant in view of the object of my visit - to learn about another shepherd of souls, now of saintly status in the Church, Father Anthony Mary Pucci, O.S.M.

* * *

To penetrate the secret of Anthony's holiness we turn to his father, Augustine Pucci, and to his mother, Mary Olive Macchi. The family lived in the tiny village of Poggiole, Diocese of Pistoia. Poggiole nestles, some twelve hundred feet above sea level, in a vale blanketed with wooded hills and studded with farms. One of these farms provided work and daily bread for Augustine, Olive and their seven children.

Augustine Pucci was sacristan of the village. He arose each day to prepare the altar. Then he assisted the parish priest at Mass, rang the Angelus, and departed for the fields. Mary Olive Pucci and their seven children followed him in this. The doctor of the town and others witnessed to the deep moral qualities of these parents dedicated to work, to prayer, and to their children. In their great charity they adopted an orphan from the Hospital of the Innocents at Florence, bringing the number of children to be cared for now to eight.

Mary Olive Pucci called all of her five daughters Mary. Her devotion to Our Lady compelled her to have the family join in saying the rosary after grace was finished following the evening meal. Often the family made a pilgrimage to the lovely little sanctuary of Madonna di Boccadirio, about seven miles away. At this spot in 1480 Our Blessed Mother appeared to two shepherd children, Donato and Cornelia. It is not unlikely that a man from Genoa, Christopher Columbus, so devoted to Our Lady, knew of this apparition.

The official registers of the parish of Poggiole reveal that Eustace Pucci was born in a house pertaining to the church and only a few yards from it. Parishioners knew his father Augustine as a "fervent and much esteemed Christian." According to Father Adolf Albertacci, parish priest of Poggiole in 1907, the family moved to another home a short distance away from the church after the birth of Eustace. His younger sister; who was still living in 1907, remembers well how little Eustace arose early in the morning to go to the parish church to serve the pastor's Mass. His sister quotes her parents as remembering him to be a good lad, years after he had departed for the religious life. "The boy passed practically the whole day in the rectory. Our parents did not let Eustace roam far from the house, or be too free with boys of his age. Mother made him work with his sisters sewing."

Eustace received Confirmation at four from His Excellency, Francis Toll, Bishop of Pistoia, September 13, 1823. According to the custom of the time, however, he was thirteen before he made his First Holy Communion. He was said to remember it as "the most beautiful day of his life."

Some days in life are too beautiful to be forgotten. So, Eustace communicated frequently and Christ nourished his life and his vocation started to blossom. Our Lady was his great love and he wanted to serve her in an Order dedicated to her service. Finally he expressed his desire to Father Louis Diddi, his pastor, teacher, and spiritual director.

Seeing the earnestness of Eustace's desire to be a religious, Father Diddi wrote to the Superior of the Order of Servants of Mary:

May 9, 1837,

I, the undersigned parish priest...of St. Michael, at Poggiole of Vernio, diocese of Pistoia, declare: Since young Eustace, son of Augustine Pucci of my parish, from his infancy even to this day, has always shown good deportment, has been and is of very good habits, has always frequented classes in Christian

*doctrine, and the holy sacraments, has been
assiduous in my school, applying himself to the
study of the Latin language with much profit and
has always given signs of a vocation to the
ecclesiastical religious state, I recommend him.*

*(signed) Father Louis Diddi
Pastor*

His father did not at first consent to his son's embracing
the religious and priestly state. However, faith and piety
overcame this difficulty, and on June 10, 1837, Eustace
entered the Order of Servants of Mary at Florence, Italy. He
was eighteen years old.

At Annunziata Monastery, the Servites served a
sanctuary dedicated to Our Lady, where the Seven Holy
Founders had first lived together. There are not many
memories of Eustace as a student. However, we have his
school notebooks. They are scrupulously kept and neatly
written. Their content gives an idea of the seriousness of his
studies. His handwriting reveals his character - open, strong
and honest. In the margins sometimes occurred such
aspirations as "To Thee alone, 0 Lord, Praise and Honor"
and "Shining Virgin of Virgins." The declarations of his
superiors on the occasion of his profession and ordination are
full of praise.

On Christmas Eve, 1837, he received the Servite habit
and his new religious name, Anthony Mary. At Annunziata,
he completed his novitiate in the section of the monastery
now occupied by the University of Florence. Throughout his
novice days he savored in his soul the power of God and the
sweetness of His heavenly glory. He yearned to shepherd

other souls to awareness of the Divine Presence - he yearned to have a pastoral role in life.

His spiritual master, Father Peregrine M. Renaggi, presented him for profession of vows of poverty, chastity, and obedience. Of Anthony Mary it is written: "The conduct of clerical student Anthony Mary Pucci of Poggiole in the time of his postulantship and novitiate has been very edifying...serene, has given many proofs of his constancy in obedience, humility and piety....He is serious and dependable.

"For this period of the life of Father Anthony I cannot do better than give you impressions of reading his writing, particularly in classic studies: that he studied as a true religious. We often found religious notes scattered and mixed in with his literary material."

On May 30,1843, he pronounced his perpetual vows, when he solemnly swore to observe forever a life of poverty, chastity, and obedience in accordance with the Constitutions of the Servite Order. He made these Solemn Vows in the chapel at Annunziata.

In the same year, 1843, Anthony Mary Pucci received Holy Orders at Holy Savior Church, Florence, on September 24. All Poggiole rejoiced the next day as he said his first Mass. Some of his family, who were with him, give us intimate glimpses of Father Anthony, the priest.

"I remember him making the sign of the cross and saying a prayer before sitting down at table. Every morning he celebrated Mass in the parish church....His thanksgiving was quite long....We saw him only at table because he always stayed in his room. This is the way he took his vacations - at home in Poggiole."

A nephew of his writes: "Every evening he said the rosary with us very devoutly. After saying the beads, he remained another quarter hour on his knees completely absorbed in God. He exhorted his mother to teach catechism and, again, to be patient with her children." This same nephew quotes the sacristan, successor to Mr. Pucci, as saying, "I never heard a Mass like that celebrated by Father Pucci." People went in crowds on weekdays to assist at his Mass because he celebrated it with such edifying recollection.

Justina Venturi said, "The Saint was very retiring, affable with everybody, and most edifying."

Visits to his family during the forty-nine years of his priesthood were necessarily rare. When asked why he did not visit more often, he answered: "I am poor. I wouldn't have funds for the trip if it weren't for a pious benefactor who helps me."

* * *

Anyone who has visited Monte Senario outside of Florence, Italy, for several days would understand how this holy place influenced the spiritual formation of Anthony. In 1234, seven young Florentines climbed the rugged hill in search of a refuge for prayer and penance. On the rocky sides of the hill cling the grottos in which they retired. Surmounting all is the chapel of Our Lady where she appeared to her faithful servants. Surrounding the chapel are the monastery and sanctuary dedicated to her Assumption. In 1727, Monte Senario was reconsecrated to Our Lady of Sorrows and St. Philip.

I have often visited this cradle of the Servite Order. Even today, Servites who dream of leading a more contemplative life retire here to renew their spirit. Anthony Mary Pucci lived here five years before pronouncing his lifelong vows, 1838-1843. In his more active life as a parish priest, he had a nostalgia for Monte Senario, the intense life of prayer, the love of silence, interior recollection, the desire of the hidden life, and self-denial.

The foundations of Anthony's spirituality were laid at Monte Senario; building that spirituality in his remaining fifty years was a challenging process. Our Lady remained the cornerstone of his spiritual life.

* * *

Following his ordination, Father Anthony could remain at Monte Senario for only a year. His Provincial appointed him assistant in the new foundation of the Order at Viareggio.

On the feast of Our Lady's Purification, February 2, 1844, the Church of Sant'Andrew of Viareggio was blessed and opened to the public. The church, begun in 1836 after many difficulties, was ceded to the Servants of Mary by the Duke of Lucca, Carlo Ludovico.

When Father Anthony arrived, the city of 3,000 inhabitants was only a rectangle stretching from the Church of the Annunziata and the Friary of the Franciscans down to the sea. The central streets around the Church of St. Andrew are the streets he knew. The Servite Priory there now is the same. So is the church. His room, located in the corner on the second floor just next to the church, overlooks the tabernacle. Adjoining the altar of Our Lady of Sorrows is a small choir now little used. Into this corner Father Anthony retreated frequently to pray during any free time he could find, day or night.

* * *

We have many witnesses of how Father Anthony lived, how he reacted towards people, how people reacted towards him. Here are a few examples.

His Excellency Sabatino Giani, the Bishop of Leghorn, spoke of him September 23,1907: "I had the good fortune to know him on the occasion of summer vacations...he knew me first as a youngster of twelve or fourteen. I stayed with Mr. Joseph Fanucci...St. Andrews Street, 12, just beside the parish church. I went every morning to the sacristy to serve Mass with his brother Giannini. This good father received me paternally, counseled me...was even my confessor as a seminarian, as a deacon, as a priest, and as a preaching missionary until 1884. In that year he made me understand that swimming for me was a luxury, so I changed Viareggio for Leghorn and soon I frequented neither one." Thus does the Bishop of Leghorn show us how Father Anthony's influence made him give up first swimming, then vacations altogether!

Bishop Giani continues, "I knew Father Anthony twenty-three years. Above all his virtues were his sweetness and kindness. A marvelous soul! But understand me well because that nasal voice of his, that monotonous and humming sound that issued forth in reading the Mass, that head bowed towards the ground, that almost convulsive shaking, these many signs that would make you think him scrupulous although he was not - these I detested. Certain colleagues of mine thoroughly disapproved. Others laughed. I could do neither. Why? Because notwithstanding this sharp censure, notwithstanding my natural repugnance to this less attractive aspect of the man, I saw, I felt that the Mass of Father Pucci was the Mass of a saint; that the glance of

Pucci, when he lifted up his eyes from the ground and fixed them placidly, serenely, and securely on those to whom he was speaking was the glance of a saint."

Father Eugene Poletti says: "Every evening when he went for his walk, we saw him caught up in prayer; when he went to the confessional; at other times as well. He prayed always."

Of Father Anthony, Brother Andrew adds: "He followed then the life of prayer. When he had time he spent it before Jesus in the Blessed Sacrament even till late in the evening."

A Servite priest of his community, Father Joseph Biondi, O.S.M., supplied this interesting sidelight in his writings: "I note this circumstance that although he knew the Psalms of the Divine Office by heart, Father Anthony held the voluminous and heavy breviary in his hands in choir, following the Office with the greatest attention. I saw it myself."

E.U. Michetti, who often served Father Pucci's Mass, testifies:

"I observed that his Mass seemed to be the Mass of a saint. His thanksgiving was long. He seemed wholly absorbed in God during his thanksgiving."

More details are given by a certain Canon of the Cathedral, Father Louis Rossi: "He celebrated Mass with great devotion, taking about forty-five minutes. He gave external signs of great faith."

Father Vincent Marraci extols his devotion at Mass further by saying, "We could not help but be edified by his Mass. In all the time I lived with Father Anthony, I never saw him omit even once a devout preparation for and thanksgiving after his Mass."

Father Anthony had a niece, Silvia Patriarchi, who said: "My mother used to tell how Eustace, at the age of only four years, was constructing little altars and lighting candles....At seven, he already served Mass. He was eager to learn about the things of religion."

Another of his servers, Brother Andrew Agnoletti, commented:

"He took a long time to celebrate Mass, but he was not scrupulous. Nothing distracted him. His manner was to make a long and fervent preparation for Holy Mass and a lengthy thanksgiving afterwards."

Julia Ghiselli revealed what the people used to say: "He distinguished himself from other priests by his great devotion at Holy Mass. You cannot be in a hurry when you go to the Little Pastor's Mass. When he celebrates Mass he seems to be in ecstasy."

Father Anthony's fervor caused him embarrassment at times. For example, he had levitation during Mass. Of this, Brother Anthony Benvenuti tells us: "During the Mass I saw him lifted up from the ground about six inches at the elevation of the host. He remained in this position at least two minutes. I saw this three or *four* times."

Father Stanislaus Borghini also saw Father Pucci lifted up during the Mass.

II. A LIFE OF LOVE
Anthony's First Love

First and foremost in the heart of Father Anthony Pucci was Jesus, the Son of God, who instituted the Holy Sacrifice of the Mass when he said to the Apostles: "Do this in memory of me." Anthony yearned to love Jesus with his whole heart and soul, with all his strength and with all his mind. The basic monastic rhythms of prayer, study, and work that shaped his life at Monte Senario now sustained him in his pastoral role. Secretly he promised Jesus to take time out daily for another side of monastic life difficult to find in a parish vineyard - solitude and silence.

He would take a sunrise walk, spend an occasional half day in seclusion, make an annual retreat. These would be his cherished pathways to his silent inner self where he could commune only with Jesus and tell Him of his love. This was his personal time to love Jesus quietly and alone. This was his time to grow close to God and to prepare his soul for Eternity.

* * *

So many remembered Anthony for his celebration of the sacred mysteries. They found him to be simple and warm in his talks to children on Our Lord's Passion, in his preparation of the little ones for their First Communion. He taught them to venerate Jesus in the Blessed Sacrament with all the fullness of their love. He encouraged processions on the feast of Corpus Christi and let the little children sing and toss rose petals en route to the church. He concentrated so intensely on the monstrance that, in procession, he never even watched where he stepped. Praise, adoration, thanksgiving and love were given by him to Jesus in the Blessed Sacrament carried so lovingly in procession.

Like David, unfolding his desire to build his Lord a fitting temple ("I have loved, Oh Lord, the beauty of Thy house and the place where Thy glory dwelleth"), Father Anthony insisted on the beauty of his church. The Mass and Benediction were to be carried out in the splendor that is Christ's due. His great concern was the upkeep of the church, and he kept it very well.

Anthony's Second Love

Mary, the Mother of God, in her role of Our Lady of Sorrows was the second love of Father Anthony Mary Pucci. As a member of the religious Order of Servants of Mary, he had professed vows of poverty, chastity, and obedience promising, as well, an unremitting service to Our Lady. Anthony loved Jesus so much that he deemed it fitting to love His Mother; too, and he vowed to serve her for life in the Order of her Servants. He seemed to sense from the beginning of his pastorate that he would save souls through her intercession. As soon as he could prepare his parishioners with the proper dispositions, he would organize a solemn consecration of the parish to Our Mother of Sorrows. In his time, consecration to Our Lady was an unusual act of devotion.

"The devotion to Our Lady especially to Our Lady of Sorrows, is something altogether special in the life of Father Pucci" said Father Joachim Ducceschi. "It appears in his little talks he delivered in her honor....

"A native of Viareggio, nicknamed 'The Coalman' - one very close to the Servant of God - told me that in his last sickness, even while he was in delirious fever, he said, 'I recommend (that you be very devoted to) Our Lady of Sorrows.'"

In his novitiate year, Anthony began an intense interior Marian life, which he was to follow the rest of his days. Each morning, early, a brother would knock on his door to awaken him, if need be, with the words *"Ave Maria"* and he would answer *"Gratia plena."* Besides the Divine Office, whenever possible, he also prayed the Little Office of the Blessed Virgin Mary. On Saturdays, in her honor, he abstained from meat. He prayed the rosary of the Seven Sorrows daily. Many recite the rosary as if reciting a mantra. His rosary was prayer. He communed with his second love, Mary, and shared in her sorrowful role during the time of Her Son's passion and death.

Each evening he gathered with his community for the Vigil of Our Lady, an ancient prayer consisting of three psalms and three lessons, together with their responses, in praise of Mary. He concluded the day by singing the *Salve Regina* and the Litany of Loreto. When the bell rang for any of these pious acts, he would take leave of what he was doing in order to be present.

In later years, after Father Anthony Pucci became superior of his community, he concluded all acts, such as meditation or Divine Office, with an ancient Servite custom. He would say, *"Nos cum prole pia,"* to which the others would respond, *"Benedicat dolorosa Virgo Maria"* (May the Sorrowful Virgin Mary bless us with her loving Child). Again, whenever he invoked the aid of Mary he almost invariably added, "Queen of thy Servants, pray for us."

Father Anthony recalled the sorrows of Our Blessed Lady to the minds of his brethren, particularly on those days which are dedicated to their memory, especially on Good Friday. Among his parishioners, rare was one who did not boast of a picture of the Mother of Sorrows in his home and on his ship.

A classic devotion to Our Lady of Sorrows is the *Via Matris.* This practice consists in making the stations of the seven sorrows of Our Lady. Father Anthony conducted this service frequently, composing the meditations himself.

When he introduced the custom of the seven Fridays in preparation for the Feast of Our Sorrowful Mother, it attracted a large following. The Feast of the Mother of Sorrows in September took on almost the importance of Easter Communion. You would see all the sailors and fishermen in Viareggio approaching the Holy Table on this feast.

Il Curatino's (The Little Pastor's) zeal for souls made him devoted to the Immaculate Heart of Mary. He asked the Archbishop of Lucca in 1852 for permission to expose a painting of the Immaculate Heart of Mary at the altar of Our Lady. In his letter he gave as a reason that he wanted it as an inspiration for public and private prayers for the conversion of sinners. Thereafter, as long as he lived, every first Sunday of the month he repeated the prayers for the conversion of sinners.

* * *

Listen now to the depositions of witnesses of his devotion to Mary. Canon Louis Rossi gives us to understand that "When *,Il Curatino* spoke of Our Lady of Sorrows, he made people enthusiastic in an admirable way. He adds further: "He sought to spread devotion to her by every means, and he was very pleased when I introduced the Third Order of Our Lady of Sorrows at Lucca."

In Anthony's time the people of Viareggio engaged in making a living mostly from the sea, and the water often showed its strength in tempests and whirlpools. The very sea that provided their living gave men the fear of the Lord. During storms, the people gathered to pray at the feet of Our Lady of Sorrows. Father Anthony led them with compelling faith in prayer for protection. Mary often miraculously saved her faithful fishermen from shipwreck. You can see the proof of this in the numerous votive offerings that cover the walls of the Chapel of Our Lady of Sorrows in Viareggio.

Father Anthony did not restrict himself to Mary's Sorrows. He prayed all fifteen decades of the Dominican rosary, embracing the Joyful, Sorrowful, and Glorious Mysteries of Mary's Life. Adele Graziana of Pistoia, age 73 in 1923, remembered: "On the occasion of the feast of the Espousal of Our Lady, certain words which Father Anthony pronounced in his discourse remain fresh in my mind: 'Just as great potentates on their feastdays are accustomed to grant favors to those in prison, etc., what will not the Queen of Heaven do for us today? Enliven your faith, dear brethren, today is a day of grace!' He would then speak on the Joyous Mysteries - the Annunciation, the Visitation - and share much of his devotion to the holy rosary with his attentive parishioners."

His Third Love

"If you love Our Lord, you must love Our Lady. If you love Our Lady, you will love her spouse, St. Joseph." Surely this was Father Anthony's reasoning. Concrete proof of his affection for Mary's husband is the lovely little oratory of St. Joseph, which he built a few yards from the priory. Witness it again in the association he founded, Sons of St. Joseph.

One of the principal associations was the "Pious Union of St. Joseph." Its object, to preserve the faith. He composed its statutes. "Give your names and especially your hearts to this Pious Union," he wrote, "and this most glorious Patriarch will present you to Mary, Mary will conduct you to Jesus, and Jesus will lead you sweetly to His Divine Father in Heaven....You will have every grace in life, assistance in death and eternal happiness in paradise. Long live Jesus, long live Mary and long live St. Joseph!"

Father Anthony proposed St. Joseph, head of the Holy Family, as the patron and model for the preservation of the faith in families, as well as Christian society.

St. Joseph, it is said, died in the arms of Jesus and Mary. Thus, the oratory of St. Joseph became the natural center for the Pious Union for the Dying. A dying parishioner could console himself with the knowledge that the Pious Union was supplicating St. Joseph on his behalf.

Wednesday was the day dedicated to the Patriarch, St. Joseph. Evil forces were attacking men's faith from all sides during this epoch. At this time, when a Jansenistic influence continued to keep many away from frequent Communion, Father Pucci invited the Sons of St. Joseph to honor their Patron by receiving Christ every Wednesday.

In sermons, Father Anthony spoke to his congregation with devotion of Joseph, the carpenter, sensitive and chaste. He told of this guardian of Our Lady who would be called "Father" by the boy Jesus. He explained with a rare understanding the meaning of Joseph's difficult destiny which was to love and protect Mary, to raise Jesus to manhood, to leave them in death that he might reach his predestined place in Heaven - to be our first saint.

III. HEROIC VIRTUE

Benedict XIV explains hope as a virtue that a man possesses when he puts his trust in God as his last end and loves other creatures only to the extent that they lead him to eternal good: (he has perfect hope) when he worships God alone, with his whole heart, with utter security, and without any doubt or hesitation, with a firmness that excludes any vain fear or over-anxiety; when he has recourse to Him alone in every need, humbly praying to Him with perfect confidence; and when in Him and because of Him he overcomes great obstacles. John Biagi spoke of Father Anthony having the virtue of hope. *"Il Curatino* instilled hope in others, keeping ever before them that we are in this world only for a short time: that we should aspire to heaven, our fatherland."

Anthony's hope that God would consider him worthy to enter heaven was neither presumptuous nor despairing. He confided not in his own merits, but in the help of God.

Lidua Ghiselli said of Father Anthony, "I believe that Father Pucci never knew impatience, so he was never disquieted or disturbed in the midst of all his parochial cares." With St. Paul's words he would hope: "I can do all things in Him who strengthens me.

Anthony was Provincial of his Order for many years. He was concerned for the welfare not only of his Order in those troubled times but also for the Church as a whole. Despite the severe trials religion was undergoing, he never despaired for the final victory over evil. "He placed all his hope in God and invoked the protection of Our Lady of Sorrows." To counteract the forces of evil in the world, he cut himself off from any luxuries. Of him, rather Eugene Poletti said: "He despised the comforts of this world and ease of life."

Cesa Biagi remarked that he told his brethren that they "must have confidence, that God never abandons them, that they must not be attached to the things of the world, riches or other goods, because these weigh down the soul as with green wood. God has placed us in the world to serve Him and to go to Him....He encouraged them to ever hope in God in such a way that he reanimated them."

His friends marveled at his charities. He was as poor as poor could be. A man lacking hope could not have dreamed of carrying out all the charities of the Little Pastor. "He comforted the poor; the afflicted, the sick and, though he was poor he distributed vast sums because he confided in God. Persons of means had such confidence in him that they gave generously, knowing that their gifts would go to the poor. Such were his alms, so endless his charities, that money and other means seemed to multiply in his hands."

Lidua Paolinelli said, "I believe that there was never more than five Lire (less than a dollar) in his pocketbook. In fact, my father assured me that when he prepared his remains for his funeral he found in the pockets of his trousers only seventeen cents."

Hope gives the saints balance and makes them even-tempered. Of Father Anthony, Sister Mary Veronica said, "I heard him say when faced with difficulties, 'God will take care of us.' He was always the same, in adversity and in prosperity."

Once he was attacked during the night, returning from a sick call, but no one heard a word of this from him. Another time, in plain daylight outside the convent, a Mason insulted him, striking and injuring him. Father Anthony did not retaliate, but proceeded tranquilly into the priory. However the people who saw the attack became agitated.

The older Father Anthony became, the more hope shone in him. To the end of his life, he worked "for the life hereafter and not for worldly glory." So firmly fixed was his hope in God that on his deathbed a witness remarked: "During his illness he not only did not complain, but he was anxious to go to God."

* * *

Adele Graziana gave the following testimony regarding Anthony Pucci: "Everything about him made you see that he had a great love for God. How I should like to love God as he loved Him."

Love of God is necessarily part of faith and hope. "Now there remain faith, hope and charity, these three; but the greatest of these is charity" (I Cor. 13:13).

Having been made in the image and likeness of the God of love, everyone has some charity within. But, to be a saint, you must desire to flee even the slightest fault against charity. Few saints have so many witnesses to their charity as did Anthony Mary Pucci.

Continual loving prayer filled the heart and mind of Anthony. "He seemed to me to be always wrapped up in God, about whom he spoke frequently...and his prayer was continuous....He tried to inflame all with the love of God."

In his activities as parish priest, the intense life of prayer, of silence, of interior recollection and self-denial were evident. Sparing in speech, he could stand in the midst of his people, his daily occupations, his numerous parochial duties, and seem to be removed from it all. He sometimes passed by people in the street without realizing that they had greeted him. '*Il Curatino* must have been in ecstasy because he didn't take notice of my greeting."

Once when he went to choir, a loose piece of cornice in the church fell on his pew with a loud bang. Father Anthony was not in the least disturbed. The noise did not interrupt his meditation.

Because the greatest moments of a priest's life are the fleeting ones of his daily Mass, it is not astonishing to find Anthony's fervor waxing strongest during the Holy Sacrifice of the Mass. As testimony abounds, it was when he celebrated Mass that he left us with the most certain signs of his love of God.

Father Hugh Tozzi met Father Anthony while the Little Pastor was visiting Siena. "I remember...that he celebrated Mass so well that people flocked to his Mass on purpose, even on week days."

* * *

The test of heroic charity is the minute observance of the commandments and counsels. A religious takes upon himself to be faithful, not only to the commandments but also to what Our Lord counseled, to be chaste, to be obedient, to be utterly poor.

Father Anthony was very observant of the Divine Law, of the precepts of the Church, and of the rules of his Order. He revealed this last when he gave his talks in canonical visitation to the houses while he was Provincial of the Tuscan province. This province includes both Monte Senario and the Santissima Annunziata, places directly associated with the Seven Holy Founders of the Order Servants of Mary.

Father Joseph M. Biondi said of Father Pucci, "He attempted to rid himself of even his smallest defects."

In hearing confessions he assisted his penitents, helping them to see how hateful sin is in the sight of God. "I am convinced that he had such a horror of sin that he wanted to avoid even its shadow." Penitents "found in him a tower of strength for inculcating horror for sin, exhorting them to purify their souls in confession. When anybody was sick...he used all the art of his zeal to reconcile them to the Lord."

"Sins of blasphemy made him suffer; he often raised his voice when God was publicly offended," commented John Dal Pino. He even had an obstinate and scandalous blasphemer sent to prison for a short time - remarkable because in this case he invoked a law which had not been enforced for some time. Brother Andrew Agnoletti observed that "if he heard anyone offending God he would be so appalled that his features would take on a different hue."

The Little Pastor campaigned against hatred of God among his parishioners as fiercely as he loved God. Julia Ghiselli said, "I believe that he spent his whole life trying to stop offenses to God and remove scandals in families. He was a bearer of peace."

Father Pucci seemed to discern the hidden causes of scandal. He could sense when a husband and wife were not getting on well. "Without being called, he would appear on the scene like an angel of peace. In the wake of his visit, discord disappeared and peace returned. Many couples living together without benefit of marriage were induced by him to have their union blessed in the Holy Sacrament of Matrimony."

The Little Pastor of Viareggio as a priest was *Alter Christus* (another Christ). "There are, however, many other things that Jesus did, which, if every one were written, the whole world I think could not hold the books that would have to be written" (John 21:25). Like Jesus, Father Anthony Pucci taught many to know God, visited the sick, consoled the afflicted, buried the dead. Both practiced charity to a heroic degree.

Pope Benedict XIV wrote: "The works of charity are threefold: benevolence, beneficence and mercy. Benevolence: to wish the person well towards whom you are being charitable. This is an act of the will. Beneficence: the good act of charity itself. Mercy: the spirit with which the act is carried out. These three became one in the life of the Little Pastor."

Father Hugh Tozzi, Anthony's successor as pastor of St. Andrew, said: "From what I heard from the people of Viareggio and from my own experience of twenty years in this parish...Father Pucci always... proved himself an excellent pastor. He converted many who told me they had been brought to God by him. He was gentle with people, no matter what their social condition, preferring to help the poor and those needing advice. Everybody spoke well of him, even those who were opposed to religion."

Of Father Anthony, Peter Larini exclaimed: "He was all things to all men. When you went to visit him, you felt that you had come upon an angel and you hated to leave him."

Raphael Ramacciotti cited an example of Father Anthony Pucci's thirst for souls. "One infernally hot day with a terrible wind from the southwest, with nobody on the street, I went to tell him that a sick patient outside the parish wanted him for confession. I suggested that he wait until this hot wind had passed, because the patient was not in imminent danger of death. Instead, he immediately departed. I stood and watched him and saw that the strong wind blew him from one side of the street to the other, but he went on his way found the sick man and heard his confession."

Anthony Del Pistoia said: "Hearing confessions neither tired nor annoyed him. He labored much for youth. He exhorted everybody to pray for the souls in purgatory."

Charity in speech is perhaps the most difficult charity. "Show me the man who sins not with his tongue and you show me the perfect man" (James 3:2).

"The Pastor of Sant'Andrea didn't want to hear evil said even of great sinners, even though he greatly detested their sins and their evil works."

Sometimes the women in the parish would speak harshly about people who had died, hinting that such sinners had gone to hell. "You are putting limits to Divine Providence," he answered once.

"He didn't seem to have any enemies because he didn't speak ill of others nor would he permit evil to be spoken of them," said Ildephonse Francesca Coni.

Although he would never have approved of the title, one witness nicknamed him "the martyr of the confessional."

A priest is perforce a public personality. This means he must be on good terms with many different groups. Father Pucci maintained good relations with city officials and various societies of the parish, civic groups and the other pastors of the city and his fellow priests. "He was deferential to all, seeking to be on peaceful and loving terms with his confreres of the other parishes."

The souls in purgatory were the special object of his charity, and he communicated this devotion to others. He insisted on celebrating the octave of All Souls Day with all solemnity. When preparing for funerals he used to tell the people, "less flowers and more prayers."

We cannot pass over his great charity for the poor, the sick, and orphans. When I was taking notes about Father Pucci at Viareggio, many came to me with stories which showed his special charity for his neighbor. Indeed, Father Anthony merits the title, 'Father of the Poor.'

In Father Pucci's time, hospitals as we know them were few. Viareggio boasted of neither hospital nor orphanage, so the sick were confined to their homes. If you were sick, you were poor. If the breadwinner of the family became ill, the family looked to the Church for food and clothing. The obvious misery of so many of his parishioners made them the special object of his charity and moved him to solicit funds and build an orphanage.

So esteemed was Father Anthony's charity that even a Masonic paper the *Corriere Toscano,* concluded the obituary of Father Pucci saying that "if it were possible to add up the charities that he had distributed to the poor it would amount to a large fortune and that he had given so much to the poor that all he had left was a few rags to cover himself."

Father Pini recounted that one winter evening Father Pucci encountered an old man in Via S. Andrea whom they called Nonno-sonno (Sleepy Grandpa), who asked for alms, "Padre...I am so cold. Can you give me a little something?"

"I haven't anything tonight," answered Father Pucci. "Turn around." Nonno-sonno turned his back and Father put his own cloak on his shoulders. When the people met Sleepy Grandpa with the pastor's cloak on they called him II *Curatino.*

Father Pucci learned that a family had need of blankets; so he brought a blanket to them one evening. The door apparently was locked so he simply looked for an open window and threw the blanket in without saying a word. By now it was the common opinion that Anthony gave everything he had to the poor.

We learn from Brother Raphael Ragazzini, a lay brother in the Priory of St. Andrew of Viareggio, that he opened the door one day to two men of the town. He did not know their names. They only said that they were there to bring help to the poor. *II Curatino* had used them as messengers since they were boys. They would bring supplies to the needy families on the pastor's list. If the families asked the name of their benefactor; he instructed them to say that it came from God and never to mention his name.

Brother Raphael continued: "A certain Raphael Ramacciotti of Viareggio told me that Father Pucci had no regard for persons when he gave a handout. The same man told that a group of young men had put on a show and had made a little money. They went to the pastor to ask him how to distribute it. To their surprise, *II Curatino* told them, 'for the moment I do not know any needy family except this particular one.' This was an irreligious and prejudiced family which was against the Church."

Like St. Vincent de Paul, who used to say "You must not offend the poor when giving them your charity," Father

Anthony sent help to a certain widow every week because she was too embarrassed to ask. Another time he called a man whom he trusted and asked him to bring some money to a needy family but was not to reveal the name of the donor.

With saints, if a noble impulse takes hold of them they act upon it without giving thought to the consequences. St. Francis of Assisi, wishing to deprive himself to follow Christ, divested himself in the presence of the Bishop of Assisi and handed his clothes over to his complaining father. Knowing the love of Father Anthony, we will not be shocked to hear then that he gave even his trousers to a ragged beggar. In Italy, religious go about in their habit, so even *sans* trousers *Il Curatino* could preserve his modesty. It could easily be that on this occasion he traded trousers, because the only pair they could find to bury Father Anthony in were tattered and torn.

The Pastor of St. Andrew's took these words literally: "Is there anyone sick amongst you? Let him call in the priests of the Church and let them pray over him, anointing him with oil in the name of the Lord, and the prayer of faith shall save the sick man, and the Lord will raise him up, and if he be in sins they shall be forgiven him" (James 5:14-15). When word came that one of his flock was sick, he was at his bedside at once, assisting him to make a good confession, preparing him to receive the Divine Physician. If the patient were in danger of death, he prayed the prayers of the dying with him; otherwise he prayed himself, till Sister Death closed the patient's eyes. He preferred, whenever possible, to remain with him until the end. "Having loved His own who were in the world He loved them to the end" (John 13:1).

The cholera epidemic struck Viareggio in 1854-1855, giving Anthony ample scope to freely expend his love for the sick. Danger of contagion could not daunt his zeal. With some of his Mantellate Sisters he gained the whole city's acclaim for heroic devotion towards the plague stricken. During this terrible time, Father Pucci slept fully clothed at the front door, ready to assist the sick and dying at any hour.

The Little Pastor of Viareggio practiced the Lord's prayer, "Forgive us our trespasses as we forgive those who trespass against us." This forgiving quality came also from his training in the Rule of St. Augustine which he followed with his fellow Servites: "Either have no quarrels or if you have them end them quickly, lest anger turn into hatred...and the brother incur the guilt of murder in his heart! Everyone who hates his brother is a murderer (1 John, 3:15)...He who will not forgive a brother must not expect to obtain the fulfillment of his prayer." The Little Pastor was prompt to pardon anybody who had spoken against him or done him injury. "Otherwise, we are not Christians," he would say.

One night he was summoned for a sick call. It turned out to be an ambush. An assailant came out of the shadows and mercilessly beat him up. Although he knew his aggressor; he would tell no one, not even the police. His confreres saw the results of the attack the next morning, his hands and face bruised and his ordinarily neat habit disheveled. To their query he answered that he had already pardoned his attacker. Only later was the assailant identified as a man who had received much charity from the Little Pastor.

Almost every facet of the great law of Christian charity shines through the life of this good shepherd. He went seeking his lost sheep. He healed the wounds of their souls and bodies and finally even laid down his life for his flock.

* * *

According to St. Thomas Aquinas, prudence is a virtue that disposes and orders means and actions to attain the ultimate supernatural end, eternal happiness, the honor and glory of God and the salvation of souls.

How does one know if he has prudence? He has if he can answer Yes to these questions:

Are you mature?
Can you say No to empty pleasures?
Are you pious?
Do you try to overcome evil desires by disciplining your body – your senses?
Do you flee the occasions of sin by work, study and prayer?
Do you keep your conscience pure?
Do you frequent the Sacraments?
Do you give God the glory for your deeds?

A prudent person seeks to give God the glory for any of his acts. This is what the witnesses in the canonical process keep saying about St. Anthony Pucci. Cesa Biagi exclaimed: "He exercised prudence, directing all to the glory of God."

Simplicity and wisdom followed Eustace Pucci from his youth to his death. He was "simple as a dove and wise as a serpent." People perceived it more after he became a priest than before. But, since no one can give what he does not have, his prudence had to be nourished with a daily diet of prayer spiritual reading, Divine Office, Mass, and the Sacraments.

Father Anthony was not abrupt in making decisions nor in his dealings with his parishioners. "His prudence knew so well how to eliminate irritating factors that destroyed the harmony that should reign among people."

If you are prudent you will be sought after. People will put their trust in you. "He showed prudence...simplicity...his counsel was valued because people placed the utmost confidence in him," said Father Sostene Guglielmi.

Thus he had a great authority over all because of his virtues. St. Teresa of Avila used to say: "If I had to choose between a prudent director and a holy director; I would take the prudent one."

"Another compelling demonstration of his prudence is that while he did not compromise with anybody in exercising his ministry, nonetheless he was much loved," Philip Dal Pino commented. Could it be because he aimed at the common good that he found it difficult to get angry?

When faced with a decision, he showed his prudence by consulting with other prudent men. He took counsel, he prayed, he acted.

It was not long before people of renown in the city began coming to him for counsel. His reputation for prudence brought lay people and clergy knocking on his door for guidance.

IV. A JUST MAN

One of the popes who suffered banishment at the hands of a cruel emperor when he came to die, summed up his passion with the words, "I have loved justice and hated iniquity: therefore, I die in exile." He was plagiarizing words that the prophet David penned centuries before in his Psalm 118. Could Father Anthony quote these words, "I have loved justice and hated iniquity?" His successor in the pastorate of Viareggio seemed to think that he could. His life "was so correct that you could not doubt his justice." Those who knew him best saw how exactly he kept his books, how conscientiously he fulfilled his duties toward God, toward his neighbor.

Father Eugene Poletti observed that the profanation of Sundays and Holy Days disturbed him greatly. "I heard him speak from the altar against certain public exhibitions and spectacles that distracted the people and kept them from going to sacred functions, especially on feast days."

So that he would celebrate Mass with dignity, he perused liturgical authors. Even the minutest ceremony for him was important. How badly he felt when through human weakness he may have overlooked some rubric during the Mass. He exercised the same care in the other acts of worship.

God's representatives must receive their due, beginning with Christ's Vicar on earth. You can find Father Anthony's devotion to the Holy See in various discourses he gave on the Roman Pontiff. Other ecclesiastical and civil superiors were also given proper deference.

His sense of justice helped him to see that honor was due to civil authority when it enacted just laws. Of course when man writes a law that is not based on Divine Law it courts disaster and it will not be observed. Why? Because the just scale of values makes citizens obey a higher law when it is opposed to a lower law. Father Anthony's wise reckoning persuaded the city council although it was against religion, to give him a free hand in distributing its public charities. His sense of justice brushed off onto the members of the council.

If authorities have rights, so do ordinary citizens. In the catechism class and from the pulpit Father Pucci taught that each of us is made in the image and likeness of God. "He gave them power to be the sons of God, those who believe in His Name" (John 1:12). In his private and public dealings with the common people, II Curatino put his conviction into practice. "He was kind and affable with all. He called people his brothers or his children. He was absolutely impartial," commented the citizens of Viareggio.

In confession a priest of God is a physician, a counselor, a father; a judge. He wishes to be a father to a prodigal son in order that he can, as a physician, heal the illness sin has brought. He must counsel with words bitter or sweet, and, using the keys bequeathed to him as St. Peter's follower; he must mete out judgment light or heavy.

When Father Anthony sat in his confessional at St. Andrew's, it was a perfect time to observe the just balance of his judgment. As St. Paul suggested to Timothy, the holy pastor did not water down the word of Christ. He urged his penitents to observe the Gospel, in season and out of season. He reproved his penitents with all patience, for he knew that otherwise a time would come when they would not endure sound doctrine, but with itching ears would take to themselves teachers according to their own lusts, who would turn them away from the truth and give them fables (2 Tim. 4:1-5).

Father Pucci, the confessor discovered the formula of a just mixture. One of his penitents, Virginia Tomei, said of him: "He was severe enough in that he wanted us to live holy and avoid even slight faults. However, if we went to confession to him with a certain fear in our heart, we came out of the confessional full of joy. For that reason I continued going to confession to him ever after."

"He had to correct me, but he did it with exquisite charity," said Father Dominic Manfredi.

It seemed right and just, since he had been called by God to be the parish priest there, that Father Anthony must bring Viareggio to that point of holiness which God's justice demanded. Faith and piety were languishing in an atmosphere of cold indifference when he came to Viareggio. By prayer, example, and preaching the Little Pastor led his sheep back to God.

Because he had a firm trust in God, Father Anthony instilled confidence in his parishioners. He had a noble expectation that, despite difficulties, good would overcome evil. God was as good as His word. "God will see to it" was a phrase constantly on his lips.

* * *

Martyrdom is an act of fortitude. For forty-five years Father Anthony endured with faith, love and patience the terrors and pains of deadly persecution. The real essence of martyrdom lies here. He stood firm for truth and justice.

Because martyrdom is suffused with charity, which is called the "bond of perfection" (Col. 3:14), it is a most excellent act. Anthony's "martyrdom" shared in the immolation of Mary, Queen of Martyrs. Mary did not die a martyr, yet merits the title "Queen of Martyrs." So it was with her faithful Servant, Father Anthony.

Cesa Biagi said of him: "I understand that he endured with fortitude the trials arising from the suppression (of his priory and community), when they carried away even the chairs and clothes. He suffered all this with patience. He was indefatigable, unconcerned about his health."

Father Pucci suffered from an obstruction in his nasal passages, for which his doctor prescribed snuff. It was not unusual even in those days, even for religious, to use snuff. He refused it. Many a night he went without sleep. As a result of this, a choleric temperament such as his would find a natural escape valve in showing irritation. He denied himself this escape. He displayed no impatience under the stress of daily aches and pains.

Whether parish affairs progress for better or for worse, its pastor must go on forever unperturbed. Raphael Ramacciotti said of the Little Pastor: "He was exact in the exercise of his ministry without, however, losing his customary calm."

As happens in the best of communities, certain of Father Anthony's confreres made no secret of their opinion of him. Yes, he had some virtues these would admit, but a saint, no. Even his prior; on one occasion, criticized him sharply without any reason. Yet not a word of complaint fell from the lips of Father Pucci.

On the 20th of September, 1870, the Rome of the Popes was captured. Orders went out that the church bells in all of Italy should be rung to celebrate this victory. Two men came to St. Andrew's and demanded the keys to the belfry. Father Pucci refused and retired to the oratory of St. Joseph to pray. Meanwhile the men forced the door of the belfry and ascended to ring the bells. They had not bargained for what happened in answer to the Little Pastor's prayers. The rope caught around the neck of one of the invaders, swinging him out of the belfry. In pendulant fashion it lifted him back into the tower saving his life. No bells were rung in Viareggio for the taking of Rome!

Father Sostene Guglielmi testified: "In the wake of the fall of Rome followed the suppression of religious orders, including the Order of Servants of Mary. On a given day the authorities presented themselves at the door of the Servite Priory of St. Andrew in Viareggio. Father Anthony answered the door and on discovering their mission he reached into his pocket, took out a document and slowly read: 'Solemn Act of Protest, commanded by the Holy See.' He was trembling with indignation as the officials carried out their mission,"

Prior Anthony's protestation did not end there, however. "In his office as superior his goodness did not impede the carrying out of justice." Whenever the political regime dared offend the rights of the Church or the Pope, he decried these affronts from the pulpit. He was not going to see his beloved people blighted with the errors and social theories which attempted to shake the very foundation of religion and faith. His courage was based on his faith and hope in God. Every morning at Holy Mass he prayed ever more fervently: "Give judgment for me, O God, to decide my cause against an unholy people. From unjust and deceitful men deliver me.

For thou, O God, art my strength, why hast Thou forsaken me? And why do I go about in sadness while the enemy afflicts me? Trust in God, for I shall yet praise Him, the salvation of my countenance and my God" (prayers at the foot of the altar).

Every day rather Anthony tried to put St. Peter's warning in the Office of Compline into practice: "Brethren, be sober and watch, for your adversary the devil goes about like a roaring lion, seeking whom he may devour. Resist him, steadfast in the faith"   (1 Peter 5:8-9).

* * *

Sobriety is only one of the many facets of the greater virtue of temperance. In a way, temperance can be regarded as a habit that disposes and inclines a person to act as his reason suggests. Because moderation is the object of temperance, we can say it belongs to all the moral virtues. It controls desires and pleasures. If Father Anthony had been intemperate, he could have excused himself even less than if he had not been courageous. His temperance was much more than shamefacedness or recoil from what is disgraceful. It was rather his keen desire to purify himself bodily as well as spiritually. As a Servite he had vowed his chastity forever. He lived temperately to preserve this vow.

He tempered his spirit by controlling his natural lust, his natural disposition to anger, and that most terrible of vices, pride. Even in his study he was temperate. He did not allow his pursuit of knowledge to descend to mere curiosity. When he walked he carried himself along as one rapt in prayer. He restrained his tongue, saving it as much as possible for conversation with God. As a religious he knew that recollection promotes discipline and union with God. Thus he always observed silence in the cloister. When the bell rang to end the simple community recreations, he retired to the choir to pray.

His was the motto of St. Francis de Sales: "Parlez peu, parlez bon, parlez bas, parlez doux": "Speak little, speak well, speak in a low tone of voice, speak sweetly."

Father Anthony was slow in asking for special food, even when ill. Friends gave him gifts of sugar, coffee, wine, but he would pass them out to the community. He must naturally have had some preferences in food and drink. If so, nobody learned what they might be. Frances Ghiselli put it succinctly enough: "He ate little."

V. SERVITE PRIEST

Religious houses have always been symbols of peace and repose for oppressed and perhaps disillusioned souls. Dante once knocked at the door of the Monastery of Corvo. The superior opened the door and asked him what he wanted. Dante was very tired. He answered: "Peace."

The religious common life, if you look at its primitive origin, is one of the most complete forms of social life. Open your Bible to the Acts of the Apostles and in the fourth chapter you will find St. Luke describing the first nucleus of a Christian community: "And the multitude of believers had but one heart and one soul: neither did anyone say that naught of the things which he possessed was his own: but all things were common unto them. And with great powers did the Apostles give testimony of the resurrection of Jesus Christ Our Lord: and great grace was in them all. For neither was there anyone needy among them. For as many as were owners of lands or houses, sold them, and brought the price of the things they sold, and laid it down before the feet of the Apostles. And distribution was made to everyone according as he had need."

In the fourth century, St. Augustine carefully tried to reproduce this vision of the Church in the Rule he wrote and in the monastic communities he founded. Many religious orders adopted his Rule, including the Order of Servants of Mary. This meant that Father Anthony had before him as his ideal the first Christian community, since as a Servite he followed the Rule of St. Augustine.

However; St. Augustine was not the only one who thoughtfully read the text of Christian communism. Today anti-Christian and atheistic communists like to cite the Acts of the Apostles in favor of their system of *forced* slavery. They do not want to see the marked differences between the communism of the early Church imitated by religious orders, and their system. Christian communism, a living together in love, is a marked contrast to their communism of hate. The first Christians and present day members of religious orders *freely* agree to work together; to hold nothing of their own, to put all things in common. Atheistic communism, by contrast, denies individual liberty and treats its citizens as so many machines united in hatred. Christian communism draws its members to God. Materialistic communism denies that there is a God to whom they can be drawn.

Although living in common, we should not immediately infer that religious attain perfection easily. Members of a religious community discipline themselves in noble self-denial and severe mortification, which sometimes reaches heroism.

"If you wish to be a religious, you desire to unite yourself wholly to God. You bind yourself to observe voluntary poverty, chastity, and obedience. You observe your holy rule."

It is not easy for a pastor of souls to follow his religious Rule when immersed in the daily round of pastoral duties. He is sometimes torn between two loves, which are only two facets of his consuming desire to love God wholly. Father Anthony Pucci realized fully that he could not communicate love of God to his parishioners unless he was a consuming furnace of love himself. He was so effective in his apostolate to souls because he was such a good religious. The abundance of God's love daily nourished by the beautiful practices of his Rule, meditation, Divine Office, recollected silence, spilled over and caught up the souls entrusted to him in Viareggio, Italy.

His success as a perfect religious and at the same time a model parish priest certainly prompted his Father Provincial to make him prior of the community of St. Andrew on May 25,1859. He gathered his new community of a dozen or so priests and brothers about him and addressed them for the first time:

"I had decided, my brethren, not to accept burdens or offices which would include grave responsibility before God and man, especially considering the difficult times we live in today. I was so persuaded and fully convinced of the truth of the axiom: 'It is better to be under authority than to command.'

"To that end I begged the superiors, both in writing and *viva voce*, that they would be so kind as to relieve me of the enormous obligations of pastoral affairs, now resting heavily upon my shoulders for reasons of health and for other grave reasons weighing upon my conscience. But the superiors thought differently, and instead of listening to me, they wished to double my yoke, burdening me with the added office of prior of this very respectable community.

"My remonstrances were in vain. My insufficiency they placed in the hands of God, so that He would give me the necessary help. And I, son of obedience, have had to submit to this difficult office.

"Confiding, therefore, in the Divine Assistance, in the powerful patronage of Mary, Mother of Sorrows, our celestial Foundress, and in the intercession of our Seven Holy Founders, I begin today, Reverend Fathers and beloved Brothers in Christ, the office of superior. A tremendous office, because I have to render a very strict accounting at God's tribunal.

"Though I know well your docility and other virtues which distinguish you, at the same time we are in a very difficult epoch, making it very difficult for me, even if I wished, to carry out my office as I should."

In these few words you can easily perceive the profound humility, unconditioned obedience and complete abandonment to the will of God shining in the soul of Father Anthony, Prior of St. Andrew's monastery. "Not to us, O Lord, not to us but to Thy Holy Name give glory."

Thanks to Father Anthony's difficulty in speaking extemporaneously, he has left us many documents in his own handwriting. One of these is the fine talk he gave to his community two days after becoming prior. It gives a perfect synthesis of what a consecrated man of God should be, a true religious in the observance of his religious vows.

"To start out on my mission as superior; I exhort you with the Apostle of the Gentiles to walk carefully along the way of the vocation to which God has called you. Then a ray of His divine light illumined your mind, made you see the dangers of the world and decide to courageously turn your back on it, and induced you to hasten to the secure and tranquil monastic order.

"Once accepted in this asylum of peace, you consecrated to the Lord the members of your body by the vow of chastity; your goods, your possessions and all your substance by the vow of poverty; your mind and your will, and your desire by the vow of obedience.

"Permit me, then, to repeat the grave warning that comes to us from the Holy Spirit through the mouth of the royal Psalmist:

"'Fulfill your vows that you made to the Most High.' For you know well, brethren, that 'It is better not to promise than, after promising, not to fulfill.' May every thought, and every dangerous affection that might disturb your peace and serenity remain far from your heart and your mind. If an ordinary Christian, is culpable when he commits sins of the flesh, religious render themselves even more guilty if they willfully mar their souls because they have not guarded their senses and (have not) run away from dangerous occasions.

"Oh, may you not be attached to the goods of this world which you have generously renounced by your solemn vow of poverty. And if you receive something for your personal use, take care that you do not become attached to it if you want to show a complete abandonment to everything that you will one day have to leave behind.

"May it never happen that you cling to your own caprice, your own will, that you interiorly rebel at commands of superiors. From these feelings spring the greatest disorders; they are deadly poison for discipline in a religious order. May the perfect and scrupulous observance of our holy Rule and Constitutions be your constant endeavor. They are the foundation stones of that religious perfection toward which we must ever tend if we value our eternal salvation."

The holy prior was aware that poor human nature stood between theory and practice. There have been, there are, and there will always be allowances made for the flesh. Even Our Lord observes this: "For the letter (of the Law) kills, the spirit gives life." So Father Anthony, with the Christ-like meekness, charity, and sense of indulgence which distinguished him, continued: "However, dearly beloved Fathers and Brothers in Christ, we should not despair or lose courage if, up to now, we have only weakly attempted to follow our sublime vocation. In spite of our ever present defects and human weaknesses, we should ever have a firm purpose of amendment, saying again and again with the Prophet, 'And I have said:

Now have I begun. This occasions change of the right hand of the Most High' (Ps. 77:10).

"In the past I was not very diligent in fulfilling the obligations of my profession. Under this religious habit, I have hidden resentment, vanity, sensuality, egotism, and caprice. In the future, I will be like a candle taken out from under a bushel and set on a candlestick, a light to my brother so that he will be edified and give glory to the Lord. When we have attained this great objective, we will be happy in time and blessed in eternity."

There you have the lofty spiritual program which the new Prior of St. Andrew's presented to his confreres. So happy to live well the disciplined life of the religious in time, Father Anthony is raised to sanctity by the Church to light our lives, candles from his flame.

* * *

Cardinal Ferderigo Borromeo once kept a whole cathedral full of people waiting because he was confessing a sinner. "Did not Christ instruct us to leave the ninety-nine sheep in the desert to go after the one that was lost?" This story illustrates how difficult it is at times for a pastor of souls to regulate his daily spiritual ministry. Father Anthony was not only a pastor but a religious as well. He followed his

Rule in order to help his sheep, which only means he divided his time with good judgment between action and contemplation. A daily schedule or rule which establishes order in either religious or civil institutions is absolutely indispensable, if they are not to fall into chaos or confusion.

"I recommend and ordain above all, your attendance at choir. No one is excepted, unless he be occupied by reason of his ministry at the hour of Divine Office." In a word, Father Anthony wanted the scrupulous observance of the community *horarium* which he was the first one to observe as an example to the community. Granted all the distractions of his busy parish life, what schedule did the Little Pastor follow ordinarily? He was up in the morning at five o'clock sharp. After his private bedside prayers, he went down to the church for Divine Office and meditation. He always celebrated the six o'clock Mass. Afterwards he made his thanksgiving for as long as he felt he could hold back the line of penitents invariably waiting at his confessional. Confessions finished, he went to the kitchen for the cup of coffee and bit of bread that he allowed himself for breakfast. Then he retired to his parish office to write and receive anybody who wished to consult with him. At the twelve noon Angelus, or shortly thereafter; he went to choir to chant the 'Hours' of Divine Office. The main community meal followed, during which one of the Fathers read aloud from the Bible or some spiritual book. Then came a short visit to the Blessed Sacrament and some minutes of recreation. As customary in European monasteries, at least in the summertime, he retired to his monastic cell in mid-afternoon for not more than a half-hour rest. Next came Vespers of the Divine Office in choir. However, Father Anthony found time between resting and Vespers to visit his flock, his sick, and his Lord again in the Blessed Sacrament.

In Italy there is a beautiful custom of calling the hour of sundown "The Ave Maria." The church bells toll for the Angelus and the evening rosary. As prior, Father Pucci insisted that all be home at this time, unless absolutely impeded by pastoral care of souls. After the rosary, the little priest went to his cell for study and prayer and expected his confreres to do likewise. Before supper, Matins were chanted in choir; followed by meditation. Following the meal there was a brief period of recreation before the community retired about ten o'clock. But the prior could not go to bed without his evening long talk with his Master, Our Lord in the Blessed Sacrament.

VI. PRIOR AND PASTOR

Father Anthony Pucci was elected Prior of Viareggio May 25, 1859, and continued in that post until June 5, 1883, a span of twenty-four years. The anti-religious Italian government had suppressed religious communities during this period making it virtually impossible to carry on the business of the Order or to elect officials. Felix culpa. Happy fault. The long regime of Father Prior resounded to enormous advantage in religious discipline and perfection for the community of Viareggio.

"Brothers," the Prior was accustomed to say, "thanks be to God, there has always existed a good, mutual harmony among us. Let us help each other and seek to understand how to compassionate each other in the ever-present defects which we all have. May our constant thought be to preserve among ourselves that peace which is the bond of perfection and the consolidating of brotherly union."

He confirmed these beautiful words by his marvelous example as superior. He wanted to lead all others in his community in his observance of the Rule. Because he was also pastor; he had to face the grave obligations to his parishioners. He therefore appointed two associate pastors with whom he divided alternately his pastoral functions. Thus he assured his brethren, his parishioners, his superiors, and his conscience that his responsibilities as prior and as pastor would be fulfilled.

In his long term as prior he kept his program intact and unaltered. He even succeeded in drawing his companions to love the program. There are members of every community who make their superior's position difficult. In St. Andrew's community, a religious enjoyed more than his share of peace, understanding, mutual compassion, zeal for souls and religious observance.

* * *

If you become a religious, leave home, father, mother, sisters and brothers, your love for your family does not lessen. It grows more noble because you have left them for love of God.

Father Anthony loved his hometown of Poggiole which he was accustomed to visit almost every year. He tenderly loved his family, and his parish priest Don Louis Diddi. Documents show that he preached in his home parish with good effect.

It was in early December of 1855 that Father Anthony received a letter from Don Luigi announcing the sudden death of his father Augustine Pucci. The Asiatic cholera had struck Viareggio. Augustine Pucci knew that many of his son's parishioners had perished. Augustine started out for Viareggio, but bad weather forced him to return home.

Biding his time, he went to gather wood nearby in Riciamboni. He was alone. Perhaps it was the humidity of the place, perhaps a sudden dizziness. Whatever happened, Augustine Pucci fell down into a little ravine striking his head against a protruding rock. There he was found dead.

Father Pucci was deeply saddened when he heard this tragic news. His father had died without the consolations of his religion. Don Luigi comforted the Little Pastor with the assurance that his father had gone to confession only the day before he died. Father Anthony's mind went back to his childhood, when his name in the world was 'Eustace Pucci.'

He thought of his place in the family of Pucci - second of seven children in the family of five girls and two boys. How dear all of them were to Father Anthony Mary. Still, all these died before Eustace, except Mary Monica. She was last to die on March 17, 1913. Mary Monica was the most authentic witness to testify about the early years of her brother Eustace.

The deaths of his mother, father, sisters and brother left Father Pucci bereaved each time. Yet, spiritually, the worst blow of his life was the death of his beloved early teacher and spiritual director, Don Louis Diddi, Pastor of Poggiole, on January 26,1861, aged 75. The now mature forty-two year old Pastor of Viareggio grieved perhaps more at this death because he contemplated the inestimable spiritual riches which the noble Don Luigi had bequeathed him.

* * *

In November, 1866, the now thoroughly anti-Catholic government legislated even more strongly in its efforts to destroy religious life. It succeeded in passing the law of suppression of religious orders, prohibiting any living in community. It confiscated goods of religious communities, forcing the members to live in the most squalid misery.

This law produced a terrible situation in Italy, similar to that at the time of the French Revolution. It gave full scope to robbery and pillage and full vent to the battle between the spirit of evil and the spirit of good. With its motto "might makes right," it succeeded for a time.

The Servite Priory of Viareggio was smitten like every other religious house. Notice was served with ironic respect upon "Mister Don Eustace Pucci," pastor of the parish of St. Andrew. His religious family and himself were forcefully put out of their home and obliged to knock on the doors of friends to beg for food and lodging.

Father Pucci was by nature timid. But his gentleness did not stop him from lodging a formal protest against these despoilers, these "enemies of God and of the Church." We have his protest in writing. Its moving simplicity speaks for itself:

"I, the undersigned pastor of St. Andrew's in Viareggio, declare that the taking possession of this Priory, carried out in November, 1866, by Mr. Delegate Parodi and Mr. Baton, Municipal Assessor of Viareggio, left nothing for my use in the parish rectory. I was treated just as any other religious, i.e.: I was given a bed, a kneeler, a chest, a table, a couch and four chairs. All other furnishings, linens, household effects, kitchen utensils, etc. were removed and locked in a separate place and eventually sold publicly by the above-mentioned persons who had taken them. The sacred vestments and appurtenances of the church and sacristy were left for use in carrying out the sacred functions of the Church, the parish of St. Andrew...no copy of the inventory, however, was given me."

(Seal) Don Eustace Pucci, Pastor

VII. PRIOR PROVINCIAL

The head of the Order of Servants of Mary is referred to as the Prior General. There are several Provinces throughout the world and over each is a Prior Provincial. The Prior Provincial oversees all the houses belonging to his Province and delegates authority to the head of each house, who is called the Prior. This is the chain of command.

A Provincial is usually a Master of Theology. He must be a man of exemplary character and morals, outstanding for his prudence and observance of religious discipline. At the time of Father Pucci he had to be at least thirty-five years of age and a professed religious for a minimum of ten years. His duty is to promote the welfare of the Province and induce all to observe the Constitutions by his words, example and corrections. He exercises a constant surveillance over the other superiors of his Province, admonishing and correcting them so that they do not become deficient in their duties. He visits each house of his Province at least once a year. He may choose any place in the Province for his residence.

In a certain sense a Prior Provincial assumes the grave moral responsibility that a Bishop has in his diocese. He must render to God a scrupulous account of his subjects.

One of the elder Servites of Viareggio spoke thus of Father Anthony: "In the thirty years or more that I had the pleasure of living with him in the Priory at Viareggio, I always thought of him as an old man." By "old man" he meant that the priest was precociously serious, prudent, and a man of reflection. At the age of sixty-four the Little Pastor was all of that.

The quality that characterized him as superior was his equilibrium, even in the most critical circumstances. Like St. Francis de Sales, his was an irascible temperament. Yet, like Francis of Assisi, he is known to posterity as the Saint of Meekness. His apparent coolness was the tempering of his intense ardor; his exterior indifference, the prudent mitigation of strong feeling; his calm, a strong shield which often warded off the imprudence of a too forward religious whom he would win over with the mighty weapon of sweetness. And here he rarely erred.

May, 1883, brought Father Prior Anthony Pucci to the heights of Monte Senario to attend the provincial assembly, or Chapter, as it is called. The three or four day meeting, presided over by Most Reverend Father Peter Francis M. Testa, General of the Order, was the first one to take place since the suppression of religious Orders. Father Anthony thought that now he could rid himself of the office of Prior.

His sense of satisfaction was premature. The assembly Fathers unanimously elected him Provincial of the Province on June 5,1883. Father Pucci, who could witness the votes piling up in his favor, knelt in humble supplication, begging his brethren to leave him free to carry on as a simple pastor of Viareggio. He pointed out that his sixty-four years of age brought with them certain disabilities hardly in keeping with such a high office. Finally the General, Father Testa, called him aside and reassured him: "When I was elected General," said he, "I didn't want to accept this high office either; because I fully recognized its grave responsibilities, but the voice of obedience forced me to accept it. Come along now and take your oath of office. I command it in virtue of the Holy Spirit and Holy Obedience." He could do nothing, as a perfect religious, but obey. Returning disconsolate afterwards to his dear Viareggio, he announced his new assignment to his parishioners: "I went to Monte Senario to get rid of a heavy responsibility. Instead they have given me a heavier one. But console yourselves, Divine Providence has allowed me to remain with you."

When he returned to Viareggio, he was stilled in heart. Here was the peaceful life he loved. The people called him their "Little Pastor" and not the more solemn title of his new office "Very Reverend Father Provincial." For this he was grateful. He dressed no differently and walked the streets of Viareggio in the same way, receiving the insults of the anti-clericals with his usual composure.

In the priory he disliked any distinction or exterior indication of his new dignity. A case in point was the Provincial's privilege of the "bugia" at Holy Mass. As for a Bishop, an assistant accompanied the Provincial with a small candle at the sacred functions. But Father Pucci was heard to admonish his assistant: "Let it be. The candle is not necessary." More important than outward signs were the commands of Our Divine Master: "Learn of Me because I am meek and humble of heart. Blessed are the meek for they shall possess the land."

We would seriously err, however, to think that his humility could not show itself at times in anger. When the officials came to despoil the priory, he reproved them energetically: "It is not for my poor self," he said, "but because you are perpetrating a serious act of injustice against the rights of Holy Mother Church."

As Provincial, Father Pucci occasionally had to raise his voice against even his own brethren who were all striving for perfection. One of them was given to murmuring. Father

Provincial, having first reprimanded him privately without avail, followed Our Lord's instructions on fraternal correction: "If they don't listen to you, tell the Church."

On a given day he called the religious into the community room and, in the presence of the assembled brethren, said to him: "My son, it's time to stop. This word going around about your conduct, which I won't call scandalous but unbecoming, must be silenced; otherwise I'll be forced to severely discipline you. Remember the obligations which our Constitutions impose and let my words be the beginning of a new life more in conformity with the rules of our Order."

This lesson in the school of perfection given with such feeling in the presence of the community had its desired effect.

* * *

It is a common occurrence that religious orders depart from their original rules and ideals, unless superiors are constantly vigilant in recalling the members to their duties. To avoid this danger every religious order lays down rules for regular visitations by superiors. As Provincial, Father Pucci visited the houses of his Province as often as he felt necessary.

What happened at a visitation? Once arrived at a priory, Father Provincial first assembled the community and spoke to them of the usefulness of visitation. He admonished them to put aside all feelings of gratitude, love, hatred, fear and human respect and to manifest conscientiously everything that should be corrected in the community. He insisted that they make known these deficiencies out of sincere fraternal charity and love for the Order; to correct the delinquent and thereby save him.

Next he would proceed to the church, examine the Blessed Sacrament and the relics of the saints to see that they were being cared for properly. He would inspect the altars and the church to see if they were kept clean and supplied with necessary equipment. Chalices and sacred vessels were checked to see if they needed replating. The stock of vestments, Mass books, and other necessities in the sacristy were examined for cleanliness and good repair. He would inquire as to whether the obligations of all Masses had been met. Were the Masses celebrated? Yes, he accounted for each one. He audited the accounts of the societies, and of the officials, the treasurer and procurator. Then he would go through the public places in the monastery and the private rooms for anything inconsonant with the spirit of poverty.

He was interested in the work carried out by his religious and attempted to assign to a community a sufficient number for the work. He was concerned about the funds set aside for the poor, or for pious works.

Father Provincial would have a private conference during visitation with each member of the community, beginning with the youngest. He wished each one to appeal to him as a father. In these private conferences he would not hesitate to inquire into minute details. In his zeal for the renewing of their spirit, he would ask, "Have the decrees of my last visitation been put into practice? Have the services in church been celebrated becomingly, with devotion? Have the members of the community frequented Divine Office, meditation, Mass? Have they observed the fasts? Is there reading during meals? Have the lay brothers and other lay persons connected with the monastery been instructed in

Christian doctrine? Do the brethren love each other? Does anybody disturb the peace of the house by his murmuring or detraction? Is silence observed? Have all members of the community, especially the sick and the old, been provided for adequately?"

If he were holding visitation at a novitiate or a house of studies, Father Anthony determined whether the novices and professed were instructed in the spiritual life, whether their studies were duly pursued, and whether they were being prepared well for their religious and priestly life. His young priests were the special object of his paternal solicitude.

Then, if necessary, Father Anthony would set down in writing any decrees for reform in the community. His chief purpose was to encourage the observance of the Rule and Constitutions. Any who were guilty of faults were corrected, publicly or in private, depending on the nature of the offense.

At the close of visitation, he would gather the community to exhort them to a more perfect life, to obedience, to mutual charity. Finally he would give them general absolution. In a word, he attempted to perform his duties of visitation in such a way that if it were possible it would never be necessary to visit the house again.

One of the Fathers of his Province said, "He seemed to come more as a subject than as a superior...he was so meek, so good; he was so mild, so affable with all, that nobody, from the prior down to the last lay brother, felt that natural nervousness or that justifiable preoccupation that a community is accustomed to experience when a superior comes on an official visit."

Flee from the world, observe your three vows and your monastic Constitutions, and above all love God and your brethren - this was the Magna Carta which Father Anthony contributed as the fruit of his six years as Provincial of the Tuscan Province.

The following is an English translation of a handwritten Italian letter sent to Our Lady of Sorrows American Province of Servite Fathers in Chicago, Illinois by Father Pucci, Provincial of Tuscany, to Father Morini, Vicar General of the Order in the United States:

"Siena, September 4, 1885.

Dear Friend and Confrere:

I answer your welcome letter of last August the 19th which came to me in Siena, where I am visiting since yesterday.

Upon my return to Florence, which will be towards the middle of this month, I will tell Father Diani, the Prior, to send you the books you requested.

The Life of St. Philip, which you translated, was printed in time and all liked it.

The Feasts have already been celebrated in Florence, Siena, Viareggio, Montepulciano, Sansepolcro, Monte Senario, and everywhere they were magnificent and solemn, and with great concourse of people. In Florence also our Most Reverend Father General was present. At all the places there were great Pontifical High Masses and grand music.

In Pistoia, Arezzo and Pisa these Feasts will be celebrated within this month of September. In Rome they will take place in October when Father General is back.

I am immensely delighted that there in America you (the community) aim at religious perfection, and that you are half saints by means of community life and the observance of our holy Rule and Constitutions; and I might add that it would be desirable if the same things would be done also in Italy. But to do so it would take religious spirit of which, beginning with myself, we do not have too much.

It is impossible to give you any Priests and Lay Brothers because I do not have any. In fact, I don't have any to send to supply the needs of the Convents of our Province.

Pray for me because I am in need. Receive my best regards and those of them whom you know here.

I am, Your Most affectionate friend and confrere,

Fr. Anthony M. Pucci, O.S.M.

VIII. POVERTY

Even as a young man Eustace Pucci desired to be like St. Francis of Assisi. True, he came from circumstances far from rich. So, if he was already poor before he took the vow of poverty, what did he really give up?

He himself asks and answers a similar query when he talks about the poor fishermen, St. Peter and his brother St. Andrew. "How much did either of these fishermen, who had almost nothing, forfeit to the call of the Lord?

"In this matter dearest brethren, you must consider the disposition rather than the personal wealth. He forsakes much who keeps nothing for himself; he forsakes much who gives up every little thing, his all. But we, on the other hand, hold with love the things we have, and even out of desire seek those things which we do not have. Therefore, Peter and Andrew forsook much when they left their nets and followed Jesus, the Fisher of men.

"What was their sustenance? A morsel of bread that they begged going from door to door and a few vegetables.

"What was their clothing? A rough tunic. And their house? A hovel thatched with leaves, or a damp cave. Their beds and pillows? The bare ground and a hard rock on which to lay their heads.

"What unheard of and almost unbelievable poverty in their marvelous example, dear brethren. Now I ask you: Who are you if not those who live on the same mountain; who dwell in the Order founded by those seven poor men of Christ, the living branches of those fruitful vines? So, then you are sons of such poor fathers; but how far removed you are from them! If a philosopher like Crates abandoned riches for human reasons, what should not religious do for the love of God?"

From his chair as superior Father Pucci preached poverty. From the height of his second floor cell he practiced it.

* * *

One of Saint Anthony's brethren thus describes the cell Father Pucci used during his lifetime: "His room was very poor. I saw it with my own eyes because I was in it many times. He had only a kneeler, a small bed, a sack filled with corn leaves for a mattress. At one time he had a small mattress, but it seems that he gave this to a man who needed it more than he. Certain it is that I never saw it again, even when I went to see him stretched out dead in his bed. Besides there were two clean chairs, a crucifix, a small bookcase attached to the wall with a few books therein, an iron washstand, and a plain desk."

* * *

While I was visiting Viareggio in June, 1962, Father Anthony's cell was still occupied by one of the fathers. He allowed me to sit at Father Pucci's desk where I wrote some of this biography.

The ceiling has wooden cross beams, the walls bare, and the other simple furnishings were as described above. The window looks out at the church and down the Via Sant'Andrea. I thought to myself, "This is the cell of a truly poor religious."

Do you think as others might have thought: "Father Pucci was only following the Rule like any other religious"?

True. Still, the Rule allows a certain elasticity in its application. Father Anthony could have furnished his room in a more comfortable fashion and still have observed his Rule. Yet he was filled with the spirit of poverty and contented himself with bare essentials.

* * *

Father Pucci was convinced that poverty is not synonymous with disorder and lack of cleanliness or hygiene. He was most scrupulous in personal cleanliness, and soap was one of the luxuries which he allowed himself. His love for neatness came from his earliest years. His room was poor; but his poverty was well ordered. His clothing was ragged, but his rags were clean. His furnishings were old, but they gathered no dust. The one who prepared his body for burial relates he found in his chest of drawers three pairs of perfectly clean underwear; but what a state they were in! The space occupied by the holes was greater than the space occupied by the cloth! "Which one should I choose?" he asked. And those who were tempted to take away a piece of his garments were unanimous in asserting they had never seen such a spectacle of misery and poverty.

During his life his confreres had to put some of his linens under lock and key, those that were strictly necessary so that he would not die of cold. Such was the warmth of his charity that he was always giving them away to the poor.

A pious and very rich lady, one of his penitents, met Father Anthony on the street one day. Noting his patched habit, she said to him confidentially: "But, Father; why don't you buy a habit that will be a little more decent? Here are a hundred Lire and pray for me." Il Curatino was confused at this act of charity, but since he was thinking more of his poor than of himself, he thanked his benefactress sincerely and candidly with: "Thank you! May God reward you, but would you permit me to use this money in the way I see fit for my poor parishioners?" The lady was speechless. She smiled and nodded her head. But, the next day, she sent the priory tailor to the Little Pastor to take his measurements for a new habit, probably saying to herself, "This time he will have to take it!" This happened a few days before his last illness, so that new habit served as Father Anthony's burial shroud.

The same thing happened to the Honorable Gianbastiani, a parliamentary official, who highly esteemed Father Anthony. He met him on the street, gave him money, and said: "Here, take this one hundred Lire note and get yourself a new habit." All Father Pucci did was thank him, smilingly, and with a few words to his generous benefactor, went on his way down the street.

A few steps farther on he met a poor widow who was looking for him, for help, with hot tears running down her cheeks. Her inexorable and cruel landlord was preparing to evict her and her children. "Fancy that, my daughter," he told her, "the providence of God arrived just in time!" And he gave her the hundred Lire note which he had not yet pocketed. Both parted smiling - this was a day of rejoicing for him.

"If one could count the money that passed through the hands and the pockets of Father Anthony Pucci during his forty-five years as pastor of Viareggio, it would amount to a vast fortune, hundreds of thousands of Lire." These are the words of many witnesses in the cause of his beatification. Money had to get out of his pocket and into the hands of his poor.

The women who did the laundry at St. Andrew's were poor people, and yet one of them, with simple logic, relates that among the bundles of laundry which the members of the community sent them, you could tell the Little Pastor's immediately! The shirts, the underwear that were patched and tattered were certainly his. "I never saw anything of his that was new," one laundress remarked.

"If he doesn't go to Heaven, nobody will," another, with a touch of impatience, said. "Charity, yes. But to deprive oneself even of what is necessary - Andiamo! That's too much!"

Now, if we would continue this long conversation with the poor laundry maids, they would say eloquently in their simplicity that Father Anthony was truly a priest of the poor. The last one who would ask him for a handout, often as not, would hear these words:

"I'm giving you the last cent I have; I would do more, but I too am poor." He wanted the poor to know that he felt what it was like to be impoverished. That alone made him apologetic when giving of his poverty.

IX. CHASTITY

For one who seeks in this world only pleasures of the flesh, St. Paul's counsel, "Seek not a wife," is an absurd aphorism that destroys and annihilates the laws of nature; but in this even the pagan Romans put him to shame, for they revered the vestal virgins with a reverence tendered to no other. Chastity is not a denial of the laws of nature. It is receiving from God the privilege and powers of husband and wife and giving them back to God unblemished and untarnished. As with poverty, we may use this world's goods and privileges. But, the less we have to use them, the higher we rise on the ladder of perfection. Some judge men and women consecrated to God by pointing out failures among them as proof that the vow of chastity is absurd. There are also persons of honest and serious demeanor who reckon that chastity is physiologically impossible. With the former we cannot argue because they are already convinced of their correctness. But to the latter we would answer: "Against fact there is no argument."

When Fr. Anthony and his fellow religious, one day back in December 1838, offered their chastity to God, this did not mean they thereby rid themselves of all temptations against this glorious virtue. Living on the heights of Monte Senario, Anthony was well aware that even the Seven Holy Founders of his Order who had lived there before him, had been horribly tormented by the instincts of the flesh in direct proportion to the horrible penances they inflicted upon their rebellious bodies.

St. Jerome, St. Augustine, and many others before Fr. Anthony had experienced the same temptations. The sure defense of purity is the fleeing of occasions of sin.

Nonetheless, undoubtedly he had his daily round with the eternal and ever present sting of the flesh. Well aware that religious persons consecrated to God were the special objects of Satan's attacks, he warned his confreres, "The everlasting enemy of God does not prefer the unguarded and abandoned stronghold, but those that are well defended, well kept, where he finds better business because the rewards are richer and much more precious." At least to our knowledge, our Saint Anthony Pucci never felt overpowering temptations of the flesh, whether from education, background, or special gift of grace. His fight was a calm and tranquil battle. It was simply that he was more passionately attached to God than to passion.

* * *

When the process of beatification had begun, we read these solemn words: *"Nulla creditur labe pollutus."* Translated this means: "It is believed that he was never stained by impurity." We have seen with how much loving care Augustine and Olive Pucci surrounded their children. They gave Eustace into the care of a holy parish priest, Father Diddi, and carefully watched the companions he played with. At the early age of eighteen he was already protected by monastery walls. As the friars filed in silently for Matins and filled the church with medieval Gregorian chant, young Eustace Pucci's vocation blossomed. He yearned to be a parish priest like his mentor Father Diddi. It is easy to imagine that he let nothing interrupt the discipline of Servite life. The lessons in modesty that he learned during his preparatory years of religious life were apparent when he became pastor of Viareggio.

Listen to how Father Pucci talked about chastity. On one occasion, he said: "Leave to the ancient and modern pagans the ignoble liberty of rendering homage to Venus, who rose as the goddess of pleasure from the foam of the sea. Leave to the lustful that follow the way of their vices, their lewd dances, nocturnal orgies, and their voluptuousness which they call 'sweetness' but which lead them prematurely to the edge of the grave and to hell.

"It is necessary, too, to avoid those equivocal words, coarse language, and double-meaning conversations; the Lord alone knows how they will finish! I will not speak about love stories. Only the honesty of the one who reads them can pass judgment here. If they honestly leave your spirit calm, go ahead and read them. But, if they inflame you, throw them away."

He pointed out that God's law of purity was simply the way to a full life, not a brake on liberty. He was capable of discussing in clear terminology the disastrous effects of breaking God's law and the deleterious consequences of habits that could become more overpowering than drug addiction.

When he spoke to his religious he recommended to them hard work and study of the Gospel, as opposed to idleness which is the father of vice and the brother of impurity. "Love the study of the Sacred Scripture, and you will not become attached to the vices of the flesh." In short, he exhorted them to the sovereign remedy of fleeing the occasions of sin and praying incessantly.

Father Anthony Pucci was minutely informed of the places and persons in his parish of Viareggio that could be sources of danger to his flock. He was particularly preoccupied with young couples. Marital life prospers, not because we wish it to but because we prepare for it. Father

Anthony Pucci had to do in his simple, non-technical way, the work of the now more developed Cana Conferences. He held in the palm of his hand the youth of Viareggio to the point where we moderns would call him a "referee" in their marriages.

One day a young girl came along to *Il Curatino* for advice. She had fallen in love with a young man whom one could only describe as a shameful scamp. Father Pucci knew her fiancé. He had seen him born, and had watched him go about in a family atmosphere that was far from promising. In a fatherly, but firm voice he counseled the young lady, looking straight into her eyes: "No, absolutely no. He is no husband for you. He will make your whole life miserable."

In a somewhat similar case he took a different approach. The girl was nineteen; the boy could not be called a model of holiness, but deep inside was a fairly good character. This time the Little Pastor called him directly and just as directly addressed him: "Listen, son, this girl loves you. She came to ask my advice. I know you well. You are not a bad lad, but your conduct is not excessively moral. This girl is so good. It would be a real sin if you were to poison her life." The young man understood, changed his manner of life, and ended by marrying happily.

Often Father Anthony warned mothers to watch over the behavior of their children, especially the older ones, what they read, how they spoke, and what places they frequented. In visiting poor homes, he tried to provide sufficient room and beds so that purity would be safeguarded. His overpowering love of chastity served as an added impulse to serve his poor.

Father Pucci had a pastoral commitment in his whole being. He saw the need of the flock to assemble with the shepherd in the celebration of Holy Mass. Divine love flowed from this Holy Sacrifice into their daily lives and so the parishioners were nourished in body and soul by the pastoral celebration. Father Anthony distributed Holy Communion as often as the Church permitted in those times. Always, he led his parishioners in prayers of preparation and thanksgiving. He gathered his parishioners at the holy table to partake of the Sacred Species representing the body of Jesus Christ, who died for the salvation of all mankind.

* * *

The political atmosphere of Viareggio a hundred and fifty years ago can be described as an anti-clerical liberalism. Good souls will always be forced to live in the midst of evil ones. "Calumniate," says Voltaire, "calumniate - some of it is bound to stick."

Morale was low, and a monastery became an object of hatred and fear. Given the opportunity to attack a priest or religious for immorality or ungentlemanly behavior; molehills became mountains. For a priest or religious to speak to a young lady was often enough matter for public scandal. It is paying a great compliment, then, to Father Pucci's purity to witness that in half a century's living in Viareggio no slanderous voice was ever raised to attack his innocence. Of his integrity there could be no doubt. He endeavored never to give cause for suspicion.

There were occasions for suspicion if anybody wanted them. Take the young Mantellate Sisters, whom he called his spiritual daughters. His relations with them might have been a fertile field for whisperings. We read only such words as:

"He founded the Mantellate Sisters, for whom he was the spiritual director. He counseled a certain Catherine Menci to found the Servants of Mary." He had to administer their properties. He had to help them materially as well as spiritually. He was only thirty-four when he began this work. What precautions he must have had to use to avoid the least slur on their character as well as his own. The Sisters came, sometimes, to meetings of his group of young people called "The Catechism of Perseverance." But once having showed them how to carry out this work of forming the young, in Christian doctrine, he contented himself to guide them only in a fatherly fashion.

When questioned about the chastity of this servant of God, Anthony Pucci, a certain nobleman, Ulysses Michetti, had this to say: "He was very modest. His manner with women was impeccable, his speech correct. When he knew that a girl had been approached by a young man whom he considered not a good Catholic, he tried to dissuade her from getting married to him. If he didn't succeed, he would approach the lad himself to help him lead a better life."

X. OBEDIENCE

Obedience is a natural imposition of the more powerful over the less powerful will. Religious obedience or Christian obedience is a free giving back to God of the highest faculty of man. It is the most perfect use of this faculty; it gives the will the fullest satisfaction because only God's immense love can satisfy its limitless craving. The individual's will is constantly being thrown off by thinking that an individual good is opposed to the Divine Will. This is a temptation. To miss loving God by interjecting one's self! For one who does not see obedience in this light it will appear hard because obedience is coercion. For him who loves obedience, it can become sweet. Christ says: "My yoke is sweet, and my burden light."

Perhaps obedience was not so difficult for Eustace Pucci. "Look at Eustace," his parents would sometimes secretly tell their other children, "he never says no." Undoubtedly Mr. Pucci hated to see his son depart for the religious life for this reason. There is an obedience that comes from virtue - this kind is meritorious. Father Pucci's obedience, like that of St. Francis de Sales, was the effect of his meditating on the virtue of obedience as depicted in Mary under the cross of Christ who was "obedient unto death, even the death of the cross." Every religious can be enthusiastic about obedience, like Father Anthony, only if he subjects his will to that of another man for the love of God - God who submitted to man out of love of man.

Very different is the obedience of Christ who invites us to follow Him. "Learn of me, because I am meek and humble of heart, and you shall find rest for your souls." Rest and peace - "the tranquility of order" - are possible only under the rule of obedience which St. Thomas Aquinas defines as: "the perfection of the religious life; for by it a man submits to man for the love of God, even as God made Himself obedient to men for their salvation."

In religious life, obedience has been called the difficult vow. So, when Anthony Pucci made his profession, he vowed "to observe obedience...according to the Rule of St. Augustine and the Constitutions of the Servants of Mary." It is in Chapter XI of his Rule that St. Augustine speaks of obedience. Here are his words:

1. Obey your superior as a father, but especially that one who has the first place of authority among you.

2. That these ordinances, therefore, may all be observed, that no disorder be passed over or neglected, but that correction be made for the strengthening of discipline, the immediate superior shall be held responsible. He, in turn, shall refer to the next higher in authority whatever is beyond his power or his right to determine.

3. Let the superior deem himself happy for the opportunity, not of exercising authority, but of serving you in charity.

4. Before his subjects, the superior shall hold a place of honor; but in fear before God, he shall be your humble servant. Let him be for all an example of good works. Let him correct trouble-makers, strengthen those who are wavering, console the sick, with patience towards all. Let him embrace regular discipline with all his heart, while imposing it with discretion upon others. While both love and fear are necessary for good government, let him endeavor to make his rule one of love more than fear. Let him remember always that he shall give an account of you to God. Whence

you also have further motives for living in due subjection, knowing that the spiritual peril of the superior is greater by reason of the heavier burden of his charge.

Monastic rules, like that of St. Augustine, have often made masters of jurisprudence marvel. Their wise simplicity, their almost perfect understanding of men, the great vision and lofty idealism come shining through the modestly written letters of the rule to create a lawmaker's legislative paradise. The founders of the great orders had no need to drown themselves in the depths of Roman Law or in the complicated science of jurisprudence. They saw, they meditated, they consulted, and finally gave their sanction in writing to rules and laws without appealing to coercive force. There were no complicated legislative commissions, only a humble assembly of wise, venerable, and prudent men. In the beginnings of the Servite Order, as I am sure with many others, there was first only the Rule to guide its members. As time went on, applications of the Rule to fit necessary changes over the centuries - applications always based on the Rule - were made. These were known as "constitutions." Rules and constitutions are, in turn, approved by Christ's Spouse, the Church, as perfect means of sanctification.

A certain pope, when canonizing a religious, was quoted as saying: "Show me the religious who observes his rule perfectly, and I will canonize him." Anthony Pucci was uncompromising in observance of the Rule.

Rummaging through the testimonials of those who lived with him, his confreres, we discover, considered him a scrupulous and even exaggerated keeper of the Rule. They even had the courage to tell him so to his face, but he was calm about it. "I prefer exaggerating a little in the scrupulous observance of our holy Constitutions to seeing some religious occasionally departing from them without any scruple. Obedience to the holy laws of the Order is a vow, and vows we cannot take lightly."

There are religious who reduce the Rule and the observance of the Constitutions to a mere bow in their direction. "Times are changed. Modern life demands different rules," they protest. Father Pucci was inflexible toward just taking the law into one's own hands.

Father Pucci knew how to command because he knew how to obey even better. In the will of superiors he saw the will of God:

"If I blindly obey the will of my legitimate superior, whatever it may be, I am sure if this be not God's will, so much the worse for him!"

Obedience is the sister of humility. Father Anthony didn't want to be pastor for fear of the great responsibility that a pastor assumes before God over the spiritual fate of the souls confided to his care. He didn't want to be prior because he preferred to be a subject rather than to command. He didn't want to be Provincial, as we have seen in the episode on top of Monte Senario during the provincial chapter.

In every one of these crises in his life, his humility was converted into obedience.

"I command you by virtue of the Holy Spirit and holy obedience." A superior uses these formidable words on special occasions when formally commanding. A perfect religious, on hearing a command couched in this language, will tremble and obey under penalty of violating his solemn vow of obedience. It would be absurd to think that a religious of Father Anthony's caliber would bow his head and obey only when formally and solemnly commanded by his superior.

His obedience followed hierarchical order. His vow of obedience bound him, after God, to Christ's Vicar the Pope, then to his religious superiors.

Not less was his veneration for the Bishop of Lucca. When I was in Viareggio, I assisted at the feast of St. Anthony of Padua, who was then the patron of the city. As an interesting sidelight on the Little Pastor's obedience, we should like to borrow the following episode from the pen of one of his admirers, Father Sostene Benedetti, O.S.M.: "Viareggio honors St. Anthony of Padua as its patron. However, in reality no ecclesiastical decree has ever sanctioned such a decision. In the time of our Servant of God, the question came up whether to oblige the faithful under grave sin to hear Mass on that day and abstain from servile work.

"Some demanded that the solemnity of June 13 should be announced from the altar every year as a holy day of obligation, and not only as a feastday of devotion. Father Pucci instead invited the people and incited them to celebrate the feast of the saint of Padua in order to invoke his blessings upon Viareggio, but did not believe it necessary in conscience to oblige them to do so and above all he did not insist that they abstain from servile work. He was so taken up with this idea that he believed it opportune to write a thesis to show with evidence that June 13 was not a holy day of obligation for Viareggio. (This thesis was guided by Father Sostene Guglielmini, a Master of Theology.)

"A peremptory order from the Chancery of Lucca intimated that he should drop the discussion, and our Servant of God (Father Pucci) immediately and amicably submitted. He promptly destroyed his thesis that he had written in good faith, and he never spoke of it again."

Perhaps you will say, "Well, even here the Little Pastor only carried out his duty." There is a vast difference between what he did in his resigned and smiling way and what we might be tempted to do in similar circumstances. We might secretly and prudently remain silent while seething with rebellion in our hearts. Archbishop Ghilardi of Lucca had a great esteem for the pastor of Viareggio. As a result of this sincere act of humility and prompt obedience, he was even more impressed with him, conferring on him the faculties, authority, and jurisdiction that ordinarily only a dean in the diocese would have.

Another example of his serene objectivity and his profound obedience to his bishop: Some pastors have become offended when their parish is divided. It is difficult to see oneself cut off from souls for whom one has been responsible. There is a temptation to pride. This time the bishop decided that a new parish was necessary in Viareggio. The Archbishop of Lucca, seeing that the population had increased, ordered the building of the new church of St. Paolino. Some of the Little Pastor's religious in the priory of St. Andrew resented the dismemberment of their parish. Father Pucci made it a point not only to lodge no protest, but gave his enthusiastic approval to the projected church, favored it, and encouraged its construction.

Father Anthony counseled his assistants: "There are, unfortunately, even in our times, persons consecrated to God who have solemnly vowed obedience, but after having vowed it do not observe it. There are, unfortunately, religious who, after having offered a pleasing and acceptable sacrifice to God - their own will - turn around with sacrilegious hands to take back from the Lord that which they spontaneously had given Him. From this originates discord in the community. From this, insubordination of one who wishes to make licit that which is not licit. From this in brief, derive perversion and confusion in the community.

"Remember, brethren and dearly beloved sons, that the virtue of obedience made God descend and become man on earth; it humiliated Him before man for the salvation of man, and made him obey even unto the death of the cross. How can you profane and trample under foot this virtue so acceptable to the Lord, that He tells us 'Blessed are the meek and humble of heart'?"

From the abundance of his heart, Father Pucci preached the obedience he practiced.

* * *

To the fourth commandment of God, "Honor thy father and thy mother." Christ added, "Render to Caesar the things that are Caesar's." The pastor of Viareggio guided his religious in the observance of their vow of obedience. He also had to guide his parishioners in this universal, binding law. Religious obedience is a law of love, whereas obedience to government is a law of coercion. At least we are tempted to regard it as such. While encouraging children to obey their parents, Father Anthony often preached on the duties of citizens towards their country.

Politically Father Anthony tended toward democracy. He shared his pastoral authority with his parishioners. He knew they could go where he could not go. They could reach souls inaccessible at all times to him. The societies he founded for youth, for the sick, for the dying, for mothers, were all attempts of sharing his authority as pastor. Though politically against the ruling Socialists and anarchists, because he was a man of order; he was nonetheless respected by them and even loved. He affirmed with St. Thomas Aquinas that if obedience is an eminently Christian virtue, it is also a civil virtue, and that every good citizen must observe the good ordering of society. Civil laws that do not offend God's laws, on which they should always be based, must be given their due, he preached.

Just as in religion obedience can be difficult at times, so it is in office, factory and shop. Father Pucci recommended to the laborers, to the white collar workers, and to the professional people scrupulous obedience to their employer. In sharp contrast to the political upheaval that was in Italy at that time, Viareggio enjoyed a kind of peace. For Father Anthony, Pastor, was a man of order, the kind of order that allows peace.

The obedient man shall speak of victory.

XI. HUMILITY

The only photograph we have of Father Anthony is from the international group of Servites gathered in Rome for the canonization of the Seven Founders of the Order in 1888. It was an indication of his humility that *Il Curatino* simply would not be photographed. The result was that his friends had to wait until he died to take a picture of him laid out in the church. This at least afforded them a picture in his new habit made a few days before his last sickness.

Father Anthony was built close to the ground in stature - barely five feet tall. In his own esteem, he was level with the ground. Yet Father Pucci was a master of theology. He was made a pastor at a very early age. He was a superior for twenty-four years. He was provincial, that is, a major superior of his Order, for six years.

This little priest was humble. He worked more willingly in the shadows than in the spotlight, in silence and in retirement, without honors and without having to listen to the flow of eulogies that were his constant torment. To hear him, he wasn't deserving at all: "What are we, brethren? We are nothing in this world, and whatever we have isn't ours. In fact, the Holy Spirit says: 'What do you have that you have not received from God?'

"O man, molded from clay and ashes, how is it that you raise yourself up so proudly? God resists the proud and gives His grace to the humble, and I assure you positively that in the sacred mathematics of grace the virtue of humility is stronger and more potent than pride."

Recently a Benedictine monk was guest in a community of friars. At table the conversation turned to food. "But we never speak about food in our monastery," he explained. "Perhaps it is because the food is unspeakable or not worth talking about." Father Anthony rarely talked about himself because, in his humility, he thought there was nothing to say.

It is known, for example, the many works thought up by him, projected and executed by him, were accredited, in his mind, to others. Foreseeing that the conversation in a group was tending toward something in his praise, he would excuse himself. One day he was at the Mantellate Sisters' Convent for Benediction. Afterwards they offered him a cup of coffee in the little reception room. The doorbell rang. Sister Mary Veronica went to answer the door; it was a well-dressed man who wanted to speak with the Pastor; and he had come to Viareggio expressly to meet him. "Come in, he is here in the reception room," said Sister Veronica. They exchanged greetings and customary bows. "Sit down," said Father Pucci.

The priest asked the man modestly, "With whom do I have the honor of speaking?" The man answered, "I've come here, dear Father, simply and solely to have the great fortune and deep satisfaction of making your acquaintance. Your name and fame and sanctity have now gone beyond the limits of Viareggio. Pardon me if I offend your modesty. It has reached even my town. Your great works of charity are known far and wide, and I have come here, as I said, to have the honor and satisfaction of knowing you, and personally offering my respects to a man who not only does honor to religion but also to his country. Your piety...."

The Little Pastor didn't let him finish. He'd become nervous with an irresistible longing to rush out the door. His new acquaintance had reached the zenith of his panegyric and Father Anthony did strange violence to his ordinarily sweet and tolerant character. Saying not a word, he left his coffee, grabbed his hat and departed, limiting himself to a reverent bow and giving the man a quick "Goodbye, Sir; I'm in a hurry."

Good Sister Mary Veronica, a little confused by it all, was left to save the situation. "Dear Sir, pardon my saying so, but I think you should have had a little more tact. Father Pucci is truly a man of God, and we can't treat man of God in that way. I apologize for Father Pucci, and he is even more apologetic than I am. I can tell you between ourselves, you are right and even we think as you do, but we are always careful not to say it to him. But it doesn't matter; what has happened has happened, and let us not talk about it any further. You have come here to make his acquaintance, and now you can go back tranquilly and tell everybody, 'I know him.'"

The stranger understood the lesson and went back home happy to have come to know a pious man.

* * *

It takes modesty in a gifted person like Father Anthony Pucci to have to deal with the poor and humble. Some of us can think of few penances so harsh as to be obliged to carry on conversation with individuals who we discover are of much lower mental caliber.

Though we cannot treat all alike, we must treat all as having the image of God impressed more deeply in them than Christ's face on Veronica's veil. For Christ says: "As often as you did it to these, the least of my brethren, you did it to me."

The poor offer us the test of our faith, perhaps more than any other class. They must have tested Father Anthony's faith even more, but he understood that poor people are often intelligent enough to understand perfectly our clumsy efforts to lift them out of the mire. "We must give to the poor," said St. Vincent DePaul "in a way that they will not feel offended by our gift." Often as not the parishioners would find their pastor down in the older quarters of Viareggio. It was common for him to be talking in friendly fashion with the fishermen. It boosted their morale and made them say: "He is one of us."

Father Anthony could never return home at night with the proud thought, "Today I have fed this family or that who would have gone hungry otherwise. I paid the rent for a family that would have been turned out of the house." No, his charity was humble, silent. If he did an act of charity, he humbled himself before God who would reward him for it. He didn't want people even close to him. Nor did he want his right hand to know what his left hand had done.

* * *

All religious orders, based as they are on the spirit of Christ, insist on Christ-like humility. The Order of Mary, named for the humble handmaid of the Lord, is exceptional in its insistence on this virtue. Father Anthony would have had ample practice in it from his novitiate on through to the end of his religious life as a Servite priest, even if he had not been inclined to this noble virtue.

Servite Constitutions insisted that the master of novices teach his fledglings: "... humility in thought and deed, according to the words of Our Lord, 'Learn of me because I am meek and humble of heart.' He shall likewise teach them to restrain their passions by mortification and custody of the senses, by a frequent examination of conscience, by menial work, and by protracted silence...to make humble, sincere, and complete confessions...how to conduct themselves on various occasions, how to greet superiors and elders, how to keep their proper place, to ask for things respectfully, to avoid haughty manner, to bear injury and insult patiently."

Every Friday Father Anthony carried out with his confreres the public act of humility called "the chapter of faults." The members of the community assemble in chapel, where, after humble prayers for guidance, one by one they prostrate themselves before the prior of the community and meekly confess in public any transgressions of their Rule and Constitutions. "Humbly prostrate in the presence of the Divine Majesty and of you, Reverend Father, I accuse myself, in my name and in the name of my brethren and fellow religious, of having failed in observance of Rule and Constitutions, especially ....For these and other faults of which I may be guilty, or which I do not recall, I humbly ask pardon of the Divine Majesty and of you, Reverend Father, a salutary penance."

The superior imposes the penance requested and avails himself of the occasion to exhort his brethren to greater fervor.

Every time Father Anthony came late into the refectory or choir; he humbly knelt in the center and waited to receive a sign from the superior before arising. Whenever he made a mistake at Divine Office, or elsewhere, he would humbly acknowledge it by reverently kissing his scapular.

He never pushed himself to the foreground except to number himself among the sinners. When he gave advice, he would say it was "from us sinners."

As superior in the Priory of St. Andrew, and later as provincial, in his sermons addressed to his brethren he remarked: "We are useless servants." Once when he was walking along near the cemetery with a friend, it reminded him of the vanity of this life. Half-jokingly, he said: "Look in there, John. When we are dead, we'll turn to dust in one plot or another."

Sometimes he encountered a bit of jealousy in his community. According to Father Eugene Poletti, Father Anthony excelled in this virtue. "I know that he had to suffer a bit of mortification from one of his assistants in the care of souls...and he showed no resentment."

Perhaps no witness gives us a better insight or summing up of Father Pucci's humility than Father Tomei, who exclaimed: "I never saw him so happy as the day he was exonerated from the office of provincial."

XII. THE PARISH

Pope Pius XII beatified the parish priest of Viareggio in 1952 as a model pastor. During his pontificate he spoke more than once on the question of the parish. After the end of World War II, for example, he addressed the pastors of Rome (March 16, 1946). Everywhere and at all times the firm foundation of the life of the Church remains zealous work in the direct care of souls, that is, the daily functions of the priest at the altar; in the pulpit, in the confessional, with the sick, giving instructions, in his personal direction and contacts. This orderly care of souls, which also includes those who do not practice the Catholic religion, is directed first of all to the supernatural life of men. At the same time, it secures the dignity, order; and welfare of human society. It is always of foremost importance, and it is the function of the parish to fulfill this task.

* * *

Pope Pius XII allowed his Pro-secretary of State, Monsignor J.B. Montini, later Pope Paul VI, to set down his ideas on the nature of the parish. In a papal letter to the leaders of the Canadian Social Week, July 18,1953, he refers to the parish as the "first and primary community of Christian life in the Church of Jesus Christ, a community conforming to man's requirements in such a way, that the shepherd can know his sheep, and the sheep, their shepherd." The parish is "the center of religious life and of missionary radiation." In this same letter he conceives of the pastor not as the head of his community in the worldly sense of the word, but as a servant of God among the faithful. Pope Pius addressed the faithful of St. Sabas Parish in Rome on

January 11, 1953. In this address he makes the goal of all parish life to know, to love, and to serve Christ. The parish community does not find its center in "the sports field, the parish theater, or even the school if there be one, all very useful and often necessary institutions." No, it simply will be the parish church, the tabernacle and the confessional. Sports and recreation have their proper place, but they must lead us back to Christ, the life of the soul, the center of the parish. Living members of a parish are recognized by their public demonstrations of faith, participation in processions, their presence at Sunday Mass, and when they gather at the Lord's table.

If Father Anthony had not lived a lifetime before Pius XII, one would think that, like St. Paul at the feet of Gamaliel, he had learned his concept of the parish at Viareggio directly from Christ's vicar, Pope Pius XII.

He believed with the pope that in the community life of the parish, Christian charity should create and further a climate of brotherhood among the faithful. No parishioner must ever be considered a stranger. He held in high esteem the other pastors of Viareggio, and was ready to help them. He could set aside the particular interests of the parish of St. Andrew, and took no part in petty jealousies as, unfortunately, his co-workers sometimes did. His commitment to his own parishioners was everlasting and his faithful found it easy to approach him with their spiritual problems.

The different societies which he formed in the parish for the women, for the men, for the young people, for the dying, were coordinated, active forces. This did not mean that there was uniformity. That would have destroyed a healthy activity which kept the objective of each real but separate. One of the deepest desires of Father Anthony was that no parish be without Catholic Action. After this, came the other societies.

There are always those men, too, who will not be organized because they do not like to be. Many of these can be put to great service if the pastor understands how to place them in effective positions of individual action. In this sense, Father Anthony used even members of the governing municipality of Viareggio. They would have lost face if they had become members of one of his parish societies, so he drafted them secretly into his works of charity among the poor.

St. Andrew's of Viareggio was the center of organized lay apostolate. The laymen, like the members of the St. Vincent de Paul Society, seemed to function under their own initiative. Perhaps they did, but they worked always under the guiding hand of the pastor who had formed them.

Father Pucci, pastor, by virtue of his office, was a natural leader of his parochial congregation and the societies of his parish.

* * *

Father Anthony is intimately bound up with the parish of Viareggio. It is fifteen miles from the Leaning Tower in the city of Pisa. Today we find it an elegant, modern city, with parks, large squares, lovely beaches on the Mediterranean. During the summer the normal population of approximately 30,000 doubles. But it was not always so.

Legendary Viareggio was probably born as a colony of Pisa back in the time of the Norman invasion of England, 1066. It was a plaything, now in the hands of the Republic of Pisa, now in the hands of Lucca, and again of Genoa. Father

Eugene Polletti, O.S.M., in his little book "Viareggio and Its Sanctuary" hints that we can't imagine more of the early history of Viareggio than we can affirm from documents. "There was the sea - there was a living to be gotten from the sea. The fishermen needed a place to live. Houses arose. Slowly a village was born." As for its name, in remote times, as far back as 1172, it was a bit of marsh land. The Republic of Lucca and Genoa were allied against Pisa and wanted easy communication through Viareggio, so at their common expense they made enormous stone blocks through the marshes, forming a practical and fairly attractive road which was called the Via Regia. This, broadly translated, meant a piece of land belonging to no one in particular except the King, *Vicus Regius* or *Vico Regio* in Italian. But, since the Tuscans often dropped "c" it became "Vioreggio" and finally "Viareggio." If you listen hard today in Viareggio, you might still hear an old-timer refer to it as "Vioreggio."

The small fort, with its tower, has been built, destroyed, and rebuilt many times over. Archbishop Arthur Marchi of Lucca one day publicly expressed his idea of Viareggio - "If I should compare my diocese to a ring, I would set Viareggio as its gem."

In the last century, Mary Louise of Bourbon, who was sovereign of this part of Italy, took the cause of Viareggio to heart. "We, Mary Louise of Bourbon," she decreed, "the Infanta of Spain, Duchess of Lucca, etc., desirous of procuring by all means improvements in the city of Viareggio, of industry and commerce... have decreed and do so decree: (1) Anyone who builds in our city of Viareggio will be granted a portion of land necessary according to the size of his building together with an equal portion adjoining for use as a garden, all gratuitously at the expense of the state and according to the conditions of this present decree. (2) The proprietors of such buildings...will enjoy for a period of twenty-five years exemption from taxes on the buildings and adjacent gardens."

When the village had developed to a sizable town, Duchess Mary Louise, on June 7, 1820, decreed Viareggio elevated to the rank of a city. Anyone can read the account on a stone in the cloister of the Franciscan Church of Sant'Angelo in Viareggio.

If we are to believe Dr. Giannelli, who wrote briefly about the city, the inhabitants were quite religious. The population rose from 3,451 to 29,300 in the space of one hundred years, 1820 to 1920. Its first church was the Annunziata, also called St. Peter's, built between 1550 and 1560. Later a church - called St. Anthony of Padua - was begun in 1624 and completed fourteen years after. Then came the church of St. Andrew the Apostle to take care of the ever-increasing population. In 1843, Mercy Church rose in the Victor Emmanuel II Square, where there is a large old crucifix that is held in great veneration. Nine years later Father Anthony Pucci built his little church of St. Joseph, of which we will speak later on. Finally there is a Church of San Paolino, the cornerstone of which was laid July 9, 1886, by Archbishop Nicholas Ghilardi of Lucca.

* * *

St. Andrew's Church might be called the home of our Saint. In this beautiful church, he prayed for sinners. In this figure of the celestial Jerusalem, as it is called in the liturgy of its consecration, he forgave sins in the confessional. Before this tabernacle he spoke long hours with his Lord.

Anthony M. Pucci, O.S.M., Servite priest, arrived in Viareggio on August 20, 1844. He had been assigned by his provincial, Father Bensi, after speaking to the prior of Monte Senario, where he had been for the first ten months following his ordination. August, the vacation month, meant a great influx of people for Viareggio. For Father Pucci, the new assistant pastor, it was an occasion to exercise his burning spirit of apostolate in the confessional. His modesty and simplicity drew the people to him. His superiors looked on. Exactly five days after his arrival, Father Dolci, prior of the community, wrote the provincial: "I wish to carry out by this letter a duty of gratitude and announce the arrival of Father Anthony Pucci the 20th of this month. I can assure you of our entire satisfaction in seeing this new priory supplied by a religious who, up to now, has given great hope for an excellent future."

This young religious was twenty-five years of age, a little man of humble appearance, who spoke not at all, and was anything but handsome. "All his glory...is within" (Ps. 44:14). Father Conti was the pastor, but he was also the assistant to the Father Provincial. This meant that he had to divide his time to some extent between the needs of the provincial and those of his parishioners. He soon learned that he could leave St. Andrew's in the hands of his assistant, Father Anthony, with a clear conscience. This went on for three years. Meanwhile Father Pucci made his novitiate in parochial life and reaped the experience that would serve him handsomely later. Somebody has called the delicate work of guiding souls "the art of arts." He studied hard; he became a master artist. A conscientious religious will never cease to study not only to complete his spiritual and intellectual formation, but above all so that he can exercise his priestly ministry with greater competence, and fill any office that the voice of his superiors may call him to carry out.

* * *

Here now is a brief historical sketch of the building of St. Andrew's Church. After the death of Mary Louise of Bourbon, Charles Ludovicus, her son, inherited the title "Duke of Lucca." The new Duke saw the spiritual needs of the growing population of Viareggio, and authorized the building of a new church on the feast of the Seven Sorrows of Our Lady, September 15, 1827. "The building that stands in Viareggio (constructed, it seems, by Mary Louise) which had been destined as a royal palace, is ceded to the commune of Viareggio, with all the adjacent property...and material toward the construction of a parochial church with a monastery attached."

The city either did not have funds or did not allocate them to begin the work. Consequently the church arose much later "in the place where it now stands, at the expense of the ecclesiastical foundation, from which were taken 30,000 scudi (official money at that time) with pontifical authorization on January 26, 1833." The design by an architect, whose name was Gheri, proved acceptable, and work on the Church of St. Andrew began in 1836. The church was completed eight years later. Father Poletti describes the church in these terms:

"The church, with its bell tower and two parallel houses stretching out behind it which served as a monastery, occupies a vast rectangular area. On the west and south there are no buildings, a fact which contributes much to its gracefulness and majesty. The Ionic style facade of white marble is supported by four columns attached to the wall.

These sustain a magnificent triangular pediment jutting out from the interior....

"Crowning the facade is the triumphant statue of St. Andrew. In the mind of the architect this beautiful statue was supposed to symbolize the greatest of the three theological virtues, recalling the divine fire which burned in the heart of the great fisherman of Galilee, for we see on each side of him two beautifully draped statues symbolizing faith and hope. All three statues are the work of the sculptor Francesco Fontana from Carrara, who carved them out of marble in 1843.

"The design of the Church of St. Andrew, as far as I'm concerned, is correct to the last detail. Some might feel, for example, that the columns are not well proportioned. This is because we are not accustomed to edifices of this architectural order...."

The church is approximately 160 feet long and 60 feet wide. It holds about 3,200 persons (standing). Entering by the main door, you get a magnificent impression.

It is divided into three naves by eight columns, which lead up to the sanctuary, with a chapel on either side forming a cross. In the middle of these rises the cupola resting on four arches...the apse is closed in by six other columns. The sacred edifice, finished in 1844, was an expensive church for those times. Against the walls along the sides are three marble altars. Eight windows in the form of half-moons light up this section of the church and six others, the apse. The main altar is dedicated to the titular saint of the church, and an oil painting showing his martyrdom is a fine work of Landucci.

* * *

Before building the church and monastery of St. Andrew's, religious had to be chosen who would service the church and govern the parish. Tradition, which seems to be confirmed by historians, would have it that Charles Ludovicus in a weak moment had favored and even adhered to certain non-Catholic tendencies. As a prince, it seems that the pope had imposed a kind of penance upon him to expiate in some way his fault. He was to erect two churches or monasteries; one of them was St. Andrew's of Viareggio.

We know, on the other hand, that Charles Ludovicus was a good Christian, thanks to the example of his mother, Mary Louise. In Lucca he had come into contact with the Servites, who had had a church there for many centuries. He loved them, and esteemed them highly. When Napoleon suppressed the friars, he was sorry to no longer have them in his duchy. He was glad, then, for the opportunity of giving them the care of this new parish, St. Andrew of Viareggio.

Another plausible explanation is found in the archives of St. Andrew's. In October 1839 two Servites, Father Nicholas Giannetti and Father Salvatore Cheli, spoke to His Highness Charles Ludovicus, reminding him of his many noble gestures toward religious. They pointed out, however, that while religious orders had now been reinstated in their monasteries, the Servites had not been allowed to recommence in Lucca. As a possibility to begin again their work in his duchy, they asked permission to begin the new parish in Viareggio. Charles Ludovicus consented to their request, and by a decree of December 22, 1839, he conceded to the Servants of Mary the church and monastery of St. Andrew.

Any history of the Church of St. Andrew must include two devotees of Our Lady of Sorrows, Joseph Di Grazia and

Caesar Sardi, one a counselor and the other a minister of state at the time of Charles Ludovicus. The first prior of St. Andrew's, Father Bonfilius Dolci, wrote his provincial April 23, 1841: "Our Order," said he, "owes much gratitude to those two gentlemen for the great interest they have shown in our favor. Now all the ministers of state favor us."

The Servites didn't wait for the completion of the church. Excited with the privilege that had been granted them, they began their fervent apostolate at once. "The church," you can read in the chronicle of the priory, "was not finished. The only part that could be used was the chapel on the side facing the sea, with a wall separating it from the rest of the church where work continued. There was a room next to the chapel used as the sacristy. Above this was space for the religious where they prayed the Divine Office."

Viareggians saw the sumptuous church arise slowly and were as anxious as the religious to see it finished. The friars, for their part, were radiant with pardonable satisfaction. The General of the Order, Father Grati, wrote the formal letter dated October 16, 1840, telling Father Bonfilius Dolci to take up residence in Viareggio as the first superior there. He arrived on November 13, but it was not until June 3, 1841 that four fervent religious, accompanied by their benefactors, Mr. Di Grazia and Mr. Sardi, together with one of the architects of the church, Mr. Cervelli, took possession of their new home. The four were Father Bonfilius Dolci, Father John Angelo Ragghianti, Father Alexis Buratti, and Brother Vincent Chiti. The annals of the priory supply us with the details. Having recited the *Te Deum* in thanksgiving to the Lord for such benefits received, they also gave due praise to the Sorrowful Virgin. The religious went to pay their respects to His Excellency Marquis Alphonse

Cittadella, Governor of the city of Viareggio. The governor returned the compliment by visiting them in person at their monastery the same day.

After midnight the people of Viareggio, who had already expressed great pleasure on the arrival of the new religious, wished to give public testimony with music and song interspersed with lively applause. Thus they openly indicated the cordiality and deep satisfaction with which the new religious were so joyfully welcomed to the city.

* * *

During his three years as assistant to Father Conti, Father Pucci found time to enrich his mind and attain an academic degree, that of Bachelor of Theology. This degree was granted at the provincial chapter of the Tuscan Province in May of 1847 at Florence. Here Father Pucci presented two theses written and developed by him. The first was entitled "Is God Provident and Generous?" and the second, "Is Unity a True Mark of the Church?" Since a student chooses certain theses, the young priest's interest in God's Providence was apparent. The second thesis may be called a major objective of the eventual pastor of Viareggio. He united his people. He saw in this unity a spiritual and material strength. Both the pastor of Viareggio, Father Conti, and his assistant were present for the provincial chapter. Father Conti was elected provincial. Realizing the value of his assistant, the new provincial named Father Pucci pastor of Viareggio.

In his humility, Father Anthony would have been happy to continue on as assistant in the parish but with humility he surrendered his will to that of his superior. The simple townspeople had already begun to call him "The Little

Pastor," and were delighted that he had been named their shepherd.

* * *

Shortly before the provincial chapter, Father Anthony became uneasy about the news from home. His mother had been ill for some time and had taken a turn for the worse. Mary Olive Macchi Pucci was only fifty-six. She was born in Gavorrano, not far from Florence, Italy, in 1791, but settled at a young age at Poggiole. At the age of twenty-five, she married Augustine Pucci. Now, on her deathbed, Mrs. Pucci was tranquil and serene. Her life was complete. The joy of having a priest son and the great feast her loving townspeople at Poggiole had made for his first Mass four years before were still fresh in her heart. Yet Father Anthony - her Eustace - arrived too late to be with her in her last hours on earth.

It was Don Luigi Diddi who heard her confession for the last time and who proceeded to anoint her while the family members assembled there looked on. Father Diddi anointed her eyes, her ears, her hands, her lips. As he dipped his thumb in the oil of Extreme Unction and applied it to her senses, he said: "Through this holy anointing and His most loving mercy, may the Lord forgive you any sin you may have committed with your eyes, your ears, your hands, by the sense of smell, or taste, or speech....Lord God, who spoke through the Apostle James: 'Is any man sick among you? Let him call in the priests of the church and let them pray over him, anointing him with oil in the name of the Lord, and the prayer of faith shall save the sick man.'" Then Don Luigi gave Mrs. Pucci Communion for the last time, strength for her final journey. He slowly recited the prayers of the dying with her: "Holy Mary, pray for her; all you Angels and

Archangels, all you saints, pray for her. Depart, O Christian soul, out of this sinful world and may the court of heaven receive you. May St. Joseph, the sweet patron of the dying, inspire you with confidence. Mary, most loving consoler of the afflicted, commend to your Son the soul of this faithful handmaid....Jesus, Mary and Joseph, may I sleep and rest in peace in your holy company"

Thus Mother Pucci died, comforted by the sacraments administered by her local pastor; Father Diddi. Her son offered the Requiem Mass following her wake. Then the bereaved priest hastened to return to Viareggio and his parishioners. Every morning thereafter he remembered his mother at the altar.

* * *

Father Anthony, now pastor of Viareggio, as a religious had to be presented to the Archbishop of Lucca for approval. In his case, approval was a pure formality because the fame of this young priest had already reached the ears of the Archbishop. Accordingly, he was approved as pastor and took formal possession of his parish on July 25, 1847. He was only twenty-eight years old.

His title, Bachelor of Theology, made him even more esteemed in the Chancery of Lucca. As a young priest who joined deep piety to solid doctrine, his qualities of mind and heart were not overlooked. Archbishop Arrigoni named him prosynodal examiner the same year. In Father Anthony's day, and as later outlined in the Code of Canon Law in 1918, the office of examiner was of great importance in the spiritual administration of the diocese. Clergy had to appear before the diocesan examiners for any ecclesiastical office. All priests, before being permitted to hear confessions, had to undergo another examination. They were examined thereafter four more years in succession for their so-called "faculties" permitting them to hear confessions. Imagine the secret envy in the diocese, when this young religious pastor became one of the diocesan examiners. His intelligence, his experience, and his piety were already recognized. But, in his humility, Father Anthony was only pleased to serve as diocesan examiner to serve the priesthood and assist the diocese.

The degree, Master of Sacred Theology, was the highest academic degree in sacred science in any religious order. Humbly, because he felt God would exact with usury the talents He had given him, Father Pucci decided to study more and become a Master of Sacred Theology, a degree given only to exemplary religious. His community would have to testify to his worthiness by secret vote.

Examinations for this degree consisted of fifty theses or propositions in philosophy and of thirty theses from some tract in theology. The candidate chose his own theological tract; from the fifty theses in philosophy he drew one by lot and wrote on it for four hours, and this was repeated the following day. If the theses were approved, the candidate was assigned two propositions, one in philosophy and one in theology, which he defended the third day. He had to prove his propositions, draw conclusions, and defend them by answering and refuting all arguments and objections. He was invited to leave, voted upon secretly by the examiners, and if he received a majority of favorable votes, he made a profession of faith according to a formula prescribed by the Holy See. Then in a formal ceremony he received the Master's Degree from the Prior General.

* * *

For three years Father Pucci robbed himself of sleep and free time to study. In 1850, during the provincial chapter of the Order at Florence, he presented the following written theses: "Should Christ as a man be given worship due to God alone?" "Is it useful and licit to abet the cult of sacred images?" "Is death the penalty for sin?" "Is the soul immortal?" "Is the state of the damned eternal?"

For oral examinations he defended the following: "Are the saints who reign with Christ to be prayed to?" "Should the Blessed Virgin Mary be venerated?" Father Pucci defended his theses admirably and was unanimously voted in by the examiners as truly a Master in Sacred Theology. The Prior General conferred the degree on Father Anthony with due ceremony. At the testimonial banquet following, the new master theologian was toasted by his brethren amid general rejoicing.

En route back to Viareggio, no doubt Father Pucci pondered:

"Now I am better equipped to communicate this deeper knowledge of God in palatable form to my beloved parishioners. Now that I have the knowledge, with God's help I will put it to work for souls."

* * *

We have described him as a priest possessed of a meek character, almost fearful. He didn't fear for the rights of man, or for himself, but he was afraid that the rights of God would not be met by himself and by others. Often in the intimacy of his cell he meditated on the gravity of his new office. "Will I be strong enough to worthily carry the enormous responsibility of all these souls? It's not the material administration that makes me fearful - it is souls that my superiors have committed to my care. They have been bought with your blood, O Christ, and woe is me if I do not make myself worthy of such a price.

"O Divine Pastor, I am nothing in your sight. You are everything. Use me as your instrument in leading your sheep to pasture."

Perhaps Cardinal Merry Del Val, Secretary to Pope Pius X and a Servite tertiary, received his inspiration from the Little Pastor. He, too, burned with desire to give himself for souls in parish work, but Divine Providence ordained otherwise. Any visitor to St. Peter's can read his desire which he ordered carved on his tomb - *"Da mihi animas; caetera tolle* (Give me souls; take away everything else)."

Another great Cardinal, contemporary of the Little Pastor, was John Cardinal Newman, who has handed down his spiritual heritage in his writings. Lesser known among his works are his beautiful meditations on the Stations of the Cross[7]. For the Fourth Station, "Jesus meets His Beloved Mother," his thoughts run their course naturally on the sorrow of Our Blessed Lady: "There is no part in the history of Jesus but Mary has her place in it. There are those who profess to be His servants who think that her work was ended when she bore Him. But we, O Lord, Thy children of the Catholic Church, do not so think of Thy Mother. She brought the tender Infant into the Temple; she lifted Him up in her arms when the wise men came to adore Him. She fled with Him to Egypt; she took Him up to Jerusalem when He was twelve years old. He lived with her at Nazareth for thirty

---

[7] Pope John Paul II used Cardinal Newman's 'Stations', Good Friday, 2001 in the Coliseum, Rome, Italy

years. She was with Him at the marriage feast. Even when He had left her to preach, she hovered about Him.

"And now she shows herself as He toils along the sacred way with His cross on His shoulders. Sweet Mother, may we ever think of thee when we think of Jesus. And when we pray to Him, ever help us by thy powerful intercession."

Father Anthony, also, could not profess to be Christ's servant and neglect His Mother. We read in the Little Pastor's writings that his first thought upon being named pastor of St. Andrew's was to solemnly consecrate his parish to the protection of Our Lady of Sorrows.

* * *

Children, though weak, have always formidable potential. God's enemies realize this, and so attempt to form children from their infancy in their evil philosophy. Herod of old had his way with children - he murdered them. Modern despots see the value of children for their selfish interests. Mussolini took the young Italians and made them Fascist Scouts. Hitler had his Junior Nazis. Stalin and Khrushchev followed suit, adopting youth to spread Communism.

As Satan works for evil, so Christ in His Church has ever wrested youth from diabolical influence by teaching love instead of hatred. Christianity has made great strides in reforming the world through its education of youth. Father Pucci, too, began his parochial mission by working with children. Priests receive some of the Church's wisdom and experience in their years of study, thought, and prayer. They cannot share it as completely as they would like. But share it they must. Thus Father Anthony initiated what was called "Catholic Action." By the second year after taking possession of the parish, he had already formed the

Congregation of Christian Doctrine, similar to present day Confraternity of Christian Doctrine.

The Congregation was scarcely erected when it went into action in sowing the seed of Christianity in the little souls. Christian Doctrine was the substance of Father Anthony's preaching, conferences and conversation. A priestly figure, combining the discipline of the Servite with that of the Italian scholar, he often admonished parents: "Send your children to learn the first truths of that faith which once sown will surely bear fruit. And, even if your children should wander from the fold, it doesn't matter. Have patience and confidence. One day the word of God, placed in those little hearts, will produce its effects. Send your children to us for instruction. Then the delusions of life will make these perhaps prodigal sons say: 'Our pastor was right. Let us return to the way of Christ.'"

One group in the parish, the children of fishermen, found it difficult to attend catechism. To teach them the simple truths of Christ, the Little Pastor would stand on the dock of the wharf in the evening and wait for the boats to come in. Then he would give them a special course, using examples from their life at sea, and in a language that only fishermen speak. At the end of the catechetical school year he gave out diplomas, but what the children looked for most were the prizes he gave the best pupils. A dear old-timer in Viareggio had a first prize diploma hanging on his parlor wall. He was quoted as having remarked: "Do you see that diploma! I assure you it's the most precious one I obtained in my whole life, including my doctorate diploma from the University of Pisa. Now in my old age that counts more for me."

Father Pucci often illustrated a true account from the life of Napoleon Bonaparte, who was born and reared on the island of Corsica, just opposite Viareggio. When Napoleon was a prisoner on the island of St. Helena, as he sat disconsolate one day, his officials who kept him company in his sad exile asked him what the most beautiful day of his life was. They wondered if it were the day of his crowning, or one of his great victories, or his marriage day.

"It was the day of my First Communion," Napoleon unhesitatingly replied.

Here is an example of what Father Pucci told little children after Communion: "Now that Jesus has entered into your pure hearts, ask Him, dear little ones, all that you want and He will hear you. Ask Him now to be good and obedient, to persevere in your faith. From this day on He is the absolute Master of your soul. You can never more abandon Him if you want to be faithful Christians.

"Today you have approached the Eucharistic table, innocent with Innocence Itself, pure with Purity Itself, simple with Simplicity Itself - children with a great Friend of children.

"Tomorrow perhaps will bring you storms, bitterness, delusion, and with it sorrow. If you are strengthened from childhood with the courage of your faith, which you find at this table, you will find here, too, the joy of hope and the anchor of salvation. But if you go about with bad companions, and if you stray far from Jesus, you will find only the desert, and, God forbid, despair."

Truly their pastor; Father Anthony, prepared the little children of this parish well for their First Holy Communion with Christ. In simple words he taught them all to be good children of God and heirs of Heaven.

XIII. FRIEND OF YOUTH

Father Pucci was a pioneer in Catholic Action. He started with the young people, following his principles; he tended toward union, organization, solidarity and cooperation, and all that had to do with the increase of the Christian religion. We see what he was driving at in founding the Congregation of St. Aloysius in his little booklet "Christian Direction for Youth," dated 1855 and printed by a printery of Florence. It is a courageous work when we consider that it was written so many years before the modern papal documents on Catholic Action. He uses Psalm 33, verse 12 in speaking to youth: "Come, my sons, listen to me. I will teach you the fear of the Lord."

"You are," he told them, "my cooperators because you can go where I cannot go. In order to be such, you must first look to the formation of your soul, because no one can give what he does not have. It is you who must spread this holy association, seeking new members among those of your friends who give solid assurance of their virtue and honesty. He continued, "I should like to see young people of our city of Viareggio, and above all the young people of my parish, giving an example to all the rest in shunning the occasions of sin which ruin the soul and weaken the body. You have to be not only hard workers, but also courageous and intrepid seamen like those who risk the perils of the sea, honestly earning their daily bread."

The Little Pastor recognized the enormous difficulties of youth. He offered a solution: "I know, too, dear boys and girls, the tremendous fight that you have to carry on, living as you do in the midst of the world. But remember that all poor mortals, especially those passing through the critical years of their youth, carry in themselves the elements and the causes of their internal battles.

"You must put into practice all the means at your command in your daily life, watching over yourself and above all praying hard. Jesus Christ has said in His Gospel, 'This kind of devil is cast out only by prayer and fasting.'

"The passions are, more than anything else, a prerogative of youth, but you must not destroy them. You must guide them. You must make another passion enter into the passion of your senses - the passion of spirit and Catholic Action. It is very natural that youth likes to associate with youth, but you must have a criterion in your choice. If a blind man leads another blind man, both fall into the pit. If, on the other hand, a blind man is accompanied by one who can see, he will walk along without difficulty.

"Flee, I insist, from companions of doubtful faith. They equivocate between what is licit and what is dangerous. You must cut short any friendship with persons of dubious character and beg Our Saviour the grace to be strong in maintaining your purity. As Jesus said to His three apostles who kept Him company the night of His Passion, 'Watch and pray that you enter not into temptation.'"

Youth needs an ideal. Father Pucci held up to the youth of Viareggio the pure example of another youth, the saintly Prince of Gonzaga, St. Aloysius, who in the midst of the elegant world of the royal court succeeded in preserving his baptismal innocence. Before becoming a Jesuit, St. Aloysius Gonzaga was a handsome page, loved and admired. Paolo Veronese, the great Italian painter of the north, left us a beautiful portrait of him.

"Try above all," he continues, "not to lead a lazy life. Keep yourself occupied with something that is attractive to you, that you have a passion for, whether it be practical work or intellectual.

"The enemy - and when I say enemy I mean the flesh - is like a roaring lion who goes about seeking to devour you. According to the beautiful expression of St. Peter: 'Brethren, be sober and watch because your adversary, the devil, as a roaring lion goes about seeking whom he may devour. Whom resist ye strong in faith."

"If this enemy finds you idle, everything is finished. You are lost. But if he finds the fort well armed, well kept, he turns around and leaves."

In thus counseling his youngsters, Father Anthony Pucci was simply following the theological expression "Grace does not destroy nature - it lifts it up and perfects it."

"My little ones," he continually repeated, "we must not be satisfied with human means which God has placed at our disposal to conquer this formidable enemy within us.

"Nothing is impossible with God. According to the expression of St. Paul, 'I can do all things in Him who strengthens me.'

"Even the great apostle of the Gentiles was tormented by the sting of the flesh. He himself relates: 'And lest the greatness of the revelations should exalt me, there was given me a sting of my flesh, an angel of Satan, to buffet me. For which thing thrice I besought the Lord, that it might depart from me. And He said to me: My grace is sufficient for thee.' There you are, children, that's what you should ask from the Lord - grace."

* * *

One day St. Dominic Savio was playing with his companions. One of them asked, "What would you do if you knew you were going to die?" Most of the boys answered: "I would begin to pray with all my heart to prepare myself." St. Dominic gave a classic answer, "I would continue to play."

Prayer, strictly speaking, is absolutely necessary every day. A simple lifting of the mind and heart to God, however; in a less restricted sense, should continue during all our waking hours: "Whether you eat or whether you drink, do all for the glory of God." Only thus can men of Catholic Action fulfill to the letter Our Lord's words: "Pray always."

"First prayer," said Father Pucci, "and then action." He did not pretend that the zeal of his young people should be absorbed by long hours of prayer, as he himself was capable of doing.

The parish priest of Viareggio explained his ideas of Catholic Action most often from the pulpit. The very ideas of this movement are in the Gospel of Jesus, which He commanded from the Mount of Olives, "Preach to every creature." In fact, Father Pucci's preaching was a form of Catholic Action at its best. Our humble servant of God was not an orator. It was most difficult for him to speak extemporaneously. He had to pass the whole night, sometimes, writing and committing his sermons to memory.

A great pagan poet wrote: "If you wish me to weep, you must weep first." When Father Anthony spoke on the mysteries of our redemption, he sometimes wept! That's what the eyewitnesses claimed. Saints' tears have a profound meaning. They mean sorrow felt. They are the effect of a mysterious and divine communion which makes a saint suffer with his Creator when he thinks of the sufferings of his Creator, that makes him weep for joy when he thinks of the joy of his Maker. He is quick to see the vanity of orators who preach themselves instead of the Gospel of Christ. It's an old story that distinguishes the Apostles of the early Church from the modern preachers who want to be apostles but cannot perceive that they must preach Christ and not their apostolic selves.

The Little Pastor desired his to be a living parish benefiting civil society. He worked hard to form the words of his sermons to instruct his parishioners on faith and morals, thus giving society a foundation upon which to rest securely. The parish supports society because it is stable; because it forms a Christian community of love; because it is a school of peace and social justice in which social differences, though they must not be ignored, are secondary; because as a community of prayer it gives Sunday its genuine, positive meaning through community celebration of Mass. With a genuine zeal for souls this shepherd brought his sheep to the fold of Christianity.

A reading of Father Anthony's discourse to the fathers and mothers of the Congregation of Christian Doctrine gives us a key to the intense apostolate of the catechism which he exercised in his parish. For him the teaching of catechism was not simply the study of doctrine, cold theory. For him to learn the doctrine of the Church was to learn how to love God, to know what God wants of us, and what we ought to do to please Him.

Here are some samples of his explanations of the Gospel, "I am the Good Shepherd," which he preached in May, 1851. "I am still your shepherd, as pastor of this church and you are my dearly beloved sheep.

"I am thereby obliged to nourish your minds with the food of the Word of God. Without this you would not be able to live very long in the grace of God, for just as it is necessary that we eat and drink in order to preserve the temporal life of the body, so it is necessary to partake of the Divine Word if we are not to fall into sin.

"I, your shepherd, must nourish your souls with the holy sacraments. Day and night I must sacrifice myself for your spiritual good. My ease, my comfort, my rest, I must give my life itself if the honor of God and your good demand it.

"But if the shepherd is so held to duty, his sheep are not less obliged toward him. Your obligation is to come and listen to me on holy days, when I announce the Gospel from the altar...the Word of God. And you may be sure that if you do not listen to me you cannot be my sheep, because sheep, says Jesus Christ today, hear the voice of their shepherd: and if you are not my faithful sheep you cannot be the sheep of the Eternal Shepherd, Jesus Christ, who said to me when He made me His priest and minister; 'He who hears you hears me and he who does not wish to listen to you neither will he listen to me.'

"You would be obliged, moreover; to provide me with the necessities of life if I had no other means... But if I am provided for; the Church is poor and needs many things. It needs sacred furnishings, linens, candles. So it is up to you to sustain it. Make your offerings for the maintenance of Divine Worship, so that Mary and the saints can be venerated in this church.

"Now tell me, have you fulfilled your obligations in the past? Have you come to Christine Doctrine class - to Catechism - to hear me? Have you put into practice what I have taught you in God's name? Brethren, dearly beloved children, if you don't wish to respect my person, because I am a sinner like yourselves, at least respect that holy mark with which I am adorned." With words like these Father Pucci taught his young flock to respect and revere the priesthood.

Here is another sample of his Sunday sermons: "You will say to me, 'Father, with God's help we are trying to do what you told us. We are trying harder than you think....We have not stolen our neighbors' goods. We haven't killed anybody. We go to the Sacraments, to Mass, we listen to the Word of God preached by you from the altar. We do what we can, and so we believe we are Christians.

"All this you say is true, but meanwhile I ask the poor and do you know what they tell me about you? They say you are an avaricious slave to your money and to your own interests, but they never receive an alms from your hands. I ask your neighbor and he answers me that you have a diabolical tongue that is very cutting...and you stir up dissension and foment discord among families. I ask your wives what you are like. With tears in their eyes they answer me it were better if they had never known you, that you abuse them, that you beat them badly, that you share your affections, your love, with other women. I ask your children what you are like and they tell me that you make their life miserable, that you frighten them, that you couldn't care less for the welfare of their soul or their body. I question all your acquaintances and they tell me that you don't steal openly, perhaps, but secretly, because you don't pay your debts, you do not pay a just wage, you use fraud and deceit, you commit sins of injustice in buying and selling. Yes, they tell me that if you don't actually murder people with your hands you do kill them with your tongue and with your heart because of your hatred, your resentment and your murmuring, that if you do not kill the body you kill the soul, which is worse, by scandal...by acting contrary to our holy religion, by following a path which leads directly to hell. They tell me that you frequent the sacraments so that you can brag about it....They tell me, in short, that you call yourselves Christians but that you are Christians in name only.

"Yes, there are many registered in the baptismal book who are registered to their greater condemnation. And why? Because one day God will judge them with utmost rigor. He will make them realize that they were baptized, that they had renounced the world but instead they have lived immersed in worldliness and have always followed the maxims of the world, that if they had been Christians they would have renounced the devil. Instead, they have served the devil rather than Christ. They had renounced allurements and vanity; instead, because of these, they have been lost."

With stirring words like these he jarred his parishioners into leading good, clean, modest lives.

Sometimes his sermons were the apologetic type. On behalf of the Church he preached: "Wasn't it the Church that overcame the tyranny and injustice of Barbarossa, that met the threat of cruel governments and tyrannical, proud and disloyal princes? Did it not attempt to reconcile people and princes, the tiara and the crown, the priesthood and the laity, and in this way make religion shine, obtain liberty among nations and international peace, concord and prosperity?

"Do you not want to enjoy that liberty which Jesus Christ gave and which the Church has always promoted and promotes? Clothe yourself with the spirit of God and you will surely have it. Where the spirit of God is, there is liberty."

* * *

In 1856 after the terrible cholera epidemic, Father Pucci consoled his faithful and encouraged them in this remarkable way. "O beloved faithful, Mary has accepted your vows, your offerings and promises as a recompense to watch over and protect you, to load you with gifts during your life and at your death, but she sets down one condition. She wants us, once and for all, to stop all this terrible blasphemy....She wants us to refrain from epithets against religion...she wants us to sanctify the Holy Days and her blessing will shower down more copiously upon our land and help us in our struggle. This is a pledge from Heaven.

"Mary has preserved your houses and blessed your fields, your affairs, your business. In her honor then, you fathers and you mothers, take more care of your children. See to their education."

* * *

Father Anthony proved to be a great preacher and a good catechist despite his handicap of not being an extemporaneous speaker. Listen to his explanation of the virtue of faith explained to adults: "After having spoken to you about the Sacred Scriptures and of holy Tradition through which God has deigned to speak to men so that they know His Holy Will and the means they must use to obtain eternal life, it is fitting that I speak to you about faith, founded on Sacred Scripture and Tradition.

"What, then, is faith?

"Faith is a gift of God and a supernatural light, enlightened by which we give our consent to all those things that God has revealed, whether they be written or not. It is called a gift of God because it is infused in the soul, without any merit on our part, without His needing any effort from us. It is called a supernatural light because our intellect, enlightened by Him, and our will marvelously submit and believe firmly and unhesitatingly all that has been revealed by God and that the Church proposes for our belief. And we see how much we need God's grace to be good, believing Christians when we say enlightened by which we give our consent to all those things that God has revealed, whether they be written or not.' I have spoken to you about the written things and I said that they are the Sacred Scriptures. I have said a word, too, about the things that are not written and I told you that they are Tradition. Through faith, then, we believe all truths, whether they be dogma or articles of faith.

"What are dogmas? Dogmas are truths revealed by God. What are articles? Articles are propositions which contain more revealed truths. The Church proposes all the dogmas and articles of faith for our belief; Jesus Christ commands us to hear her as we would hear Himself because He has established her as the pillar and foundation of truth and consequently she cannot err when she proposes something regarding faith, morals or discipline.

"Faith is of various kinds. There is habitual and actual faith, implicit and explicit faith, internal and external faith, living and dead faith. Habitual faith is infused in the soul through holy Baptism."

* * *

And so, to the youth and to the grown-ups, the Little Pastor preached faith, hope and charity. He renewed in his parishioners fervor for their religion in a spirit which anticipated the liturgical movement.

In 1925 the famous Ildefonse Herwegen wrote an article entitled "Liturgical Renewal and the Renewal of the Apostolate" which said: "The intimate participation of the laity in the liturgy is the best means to restore the parish to its proper place in orderly pastoral care."

Even before Abbot Herwegen, much had been written about the relation between liturgy and parish. The liturgical movement began with the formation of small study groups. It developed into youth movements that dominated the liturgical movement. Finally, it came to the parish and its goal was to create living parishes, worshiping in common.

The liturgical movement, from its beginning, aimed at restoring knowledge of the Holy Scriptures to a rightful place in the lives of the faithful. Father Pius Parsch and his followers especially dedicated themselves to this work.

The sermons of Father Anthony Pucci interestingly enough followed this pattern. Mostly, they comment on Christ's life as relived in the course of the liturgical year. His Mass, the proclamation of Christ's death, the celebration of the Lord's Supper, which He commanded to be carried out in memory of Him, was a sermon in itself. His discourse was prophetic because he saw himself only as God's instrument.

As a Servite priest, Father Anthony had been brought up spiritually on the doctrine of St. Augustine's Rule. Now, as everybody knows, St. Augustine only tried to establish a Christian life like the community of Christians in the New Testament. This idea of early Christian community living

Anthony Pucci essayed to translate into his parish of Viareggio. He saw his people not just as a religious association but as a social grouping. He tried to unite his disengaged and separated members of the parish to one another by his personal relationship with them. He united them and their interests and invited them to love their parish as their home.

XIV. PAROCHIAL ASSOCIATIONS

At his arrival in Viareggio, the Company of Our Lady of Sorrows for Men, who helped in parish work, had scarcely been started. Besides encouraging them to a holy life, Father Anthony insisted on their receiving the sacraments frequently and exercising works of mercy in their parish. It was with the help of these men that Father Pucci erected the oratory or smaller church of St. Joseph (1852) which became the center of the social action of the parish.

The year 1850 saw the foundation of the Company of St. Aloysius Gonzaga for young people. Generally such organizations limited themselves to devotion toward their patron and solemnizing his feast. Instead, Father Anthony's idea or intention was to foster in young people an integral Catholic life and social apostolate. To illustrate this point and to understand how the Little Pastor was a farseeing forerunner of our present day apostolate of the laity, it suffices to run over the chapter headings of the Rule of the Company of St. Aloysius, which he wrote:

1. That we must make war on ourselves if we are to acquire Christian virtues.

2. That we must deny our own will, our own passions, seek to hunger after God and flee idleness.

3. That we must resist temptation.

4. That we must have a low opinion of ourselves and not mix ourselves too easily into the affairs of others, and be content with little.

5. How to conduct ourselves with our parents or other superiors.

6. We must love our neighbor.

7. We must pray, and how we must pray and meditate.

8. We must often examine our own conscience.

9. We must go to Confession often and the disposition for Confession.

10. We must receive Communion, and what our dispositions should be.

11. The precious time after Communion.

12. How we should behave in church.

13. We must find a good companion and flee the company of the bad.

14. We must not read bad books.

15. We should flee the horrible monster of blasphemy and sanctify Holy Days.

16. We must have devotion to the Immaculate Virgin.

17. We must profess devotion to the Angels and Saints of Heaven.

At the end he recommends some aspirations directed to Jesus, a prayer to Our Lady of Sorrows, and a prayer to St. Aloysius Gonzaga.

* * *

Around 1860, Father Anthony Pucci founded the Pious Union of the Children of St. Joseph "to solidify the Catholic faith in families and Christian society." Its rule, approved by the Archbishop of Lucca in 1877, is a little masterpiece of spiritual and social direction founded on devotion to the Holy Family. While the Company of Our Lady of Sorrows provided spiritual formation for the adults called to collaborate with the pastor, in the parish itself, and the Company of St. Aloysius followed the same lines in spiritual formation of the young people, the Pious Union of the Children of St. Joseph, to which all could belong, had a double scope: to sanctify one's own family and so strengthen the internal structure of Christianity and to work for the sanctification of other families by means of edifying them, by works of charity, loving the poor; helping them, exhorting them to patience, and carrying out God's will.

What induced Father Anthony to institute the Pious Union? The Little Pastor wanted "to arrest the torrent of immorality, of evil doctrine and bad example which shakes the whole society to its foundations and threatens to ruin it. To obviate such a catastrophe and maintain in the Christian families a persevering and working faith, sound and unblemished, as professed in holy baptism." The Christian knows through faith that suffering has meaning.

Conditions for admission into the Pious Union (besides the forty cents annually) were to inscribe "the children in a Congregation of Christian Doctrine; the adults must come to Christian Doctrine course and to Catechism on Sundays and evenings. They must, moreover; at the request of the parish priest, agree to act as instructors in Christian Doctrine to the boys and girls, see that all maintained order in the church, see that they were all devout as the holy place demands; and while they listened to the Word of God to be not distracted but attentively and carefully try to learn what is necessary that a Christian know in order to gain eternal salvation."

Here are some of the Articles of the Rule of Life of the Pious Union. Notice Father Anthony's insistence on using the means to increase holiness in the family and to resist the evil practices and revolutionary heretical and atheistic theories of the time.

1. The children of the Pious Union will seek daily to honor the Holy Family of Jesus, Mary and Joseph in their prayers, aspirations and ejaculations, and especially imitating their example and virtue.

2. They will be exact in carrying out their duties, taking care that the whole family live in a Christian manner, and at least in the evening recite in common the following prayer: 'Jesus, Mary and Joseph, help us. Assist us always in life and in death!'

3. They will keep far from their houses any dangerous objects such as indecent pictures, bad novels, condemned books and newspapers that contaminate hearts, corrupt morals, and make even good people vacillate in their right belief.

4. They will apply themselves to maintaining fraternal union, not using any indecent, scandalous, or harmful words.

5. By their example they will take care to lead all the members of their family in the exact observance of the commandments of God, the precepts of the Church, and especially the sanctification of Holy Days, the observance of Fridays and Saturdays, and Easter Confession and Communion.

6. They will resist the false maxims of the world, the impious and heretical suggestions of melancholy and stupid people and all the forces which create hell in our times, seeking to break up families and render both

parents and children negligent in the practice of their most essential duties.

7. They will make everyone love their family life, in the midst of Jesus, Mary and Joseph, maintaining order, cleanliness, decency, reading occasionally interesting and pious books, and sometimes giving themselves to parties and honest recreation.

8. They shall form edifying and charitable relations with other families. They shall love the poor, sick, afflicted; helping them in their need and exhorting them to patience and to carry out the will of God.

9. Among the other devotions, the Children of St. Joseph will prefer those of the Most Blessed Sacrament, the Sacred Heart of Jesus, the month of January dedicated to the Infant Jesus, meditation on the passion and death of our Divine Redeemer; those of Our Lady, especially the Immaculate Conception, her purity and virginity, and her piercing sorrows; and those of our Holy Patriarch; they should go to church often but particularly on Wednesdays; they will send up heartfelt prayers for themselves, for their families, for the many needs of Holy Roman Church, for the conversion of sinners; receive, so far as possible, Communion on Wednesdays; celebrate his feast...and honor the thirty years which St. Joseph lived with Jesus and Mary.

10. They shall attempt, so far as they can, to spread devotion to this great saint and gain the indulgences granted to this Pious Union for their own souls, the souls in Purgatory - particularly their deceased parents and associates. They shall consecrate themselves and their families to the Holy Patriarch.

* * *

Frederick Ozanam, the founder of the Conference of St. Vincent de Paul, died in 1853. That very year Father Pucci gathered around himself a group of choice parishioners to begin the first Conference of St. Vincent de Paul at Viareggio. We still have the notes of the talk he gave those men. He expressed his happiness at seeing such a large group of men filled with holy desire to help the poor families each week.

Another activity to which Father Anthony dedicated his zeal was the work of the Association of the Holy Childhood and the Propagation of the Faith. His parish was always first with contributions in the diocese. He distributed the Annals of the Propagation of the Faith and gathered the associates into groups which he addressed every so often to enkindle the love of missions.

He did even more for the Association of the Holy Childhood by inscribing as many children as he could. He held meetings frequently and spoke to them of the sad lot of the Chinese babies. He got them to save up their pennies to preserve the lives of these little children. He asked John Pacini of Viareggio, who was a master musician, to compose a hymn to the Holy Childhood. The solo part, taken by a would-be Christian baby, incites pity, enumerating all the benefits of faith and family that he and his little friends do not have. The choir (the Catholic babies) answer him, assuring the baby that they will make every sacrifice to help him. Since we do not know the author of the words, we can give Father Anthony credit for the sentiments. The Hymn to the Holy Childhood was later printed by Father Anthony and taken up by other churches of the Order.

* * *

Forty years before Anthony Pucci died, the providence of God had given him a group of fervent young ladies. One of these, Catherine Lenci, decided that she was destined for the cloister and departed for Lucca. Her health was very delicate so she had to return in a short time. The Little Pastor encouraged her; saying that she should await the Lord's word with calm, praying Him to render her worthy of His merciful light by trying to lead a holier life.

Meanwhile, the young Catherine, with three other friends, became inflamed with a great desire to consecrate themselves to the service of Our Lady and she asked the pastor if he would admit the four of them into the Servite Third Order of Our Lady. So, Father Anthony invested them with the habit, and, after one year in the novitiate, received their profession. They remained closely bound to his work.

The last step came almost by itself. Catherine had never lost the desire for religious life. She wanted to link her life more intimately with her three companions. This inspired her to ask the Little Pastor if they could be together in a house and begin to have a common life in order to dedicate themselves to good works under his authority. He prayed much over this, then asked his superiors' opinions. Finally, Father Anthony granted them permission.

Practically every afternoon thereafter he went to the Sisters' house to visit, to encourage, and to direct them. He remained their spiritual director for many years. Their institute remained dependent on the superiors of the Order of Servants of Mary until 1886. That year the Sisters presented their Rule to the Chancery of Lucca for ecclesiastical approbation. The foundress, now Sister Juliana Lenci, was devoted to the pastor and did hardly anything without his consent. So the great work of charity that these Sisters eventually carried out, their utter dependence on God, and their spirit of sacrifice and love must be attributed in great part to Father Anthony's counsel and impulse. On April 7, 1886, Father Pucci wrote to his confreres in Chicago about the Sisters. The following letter was to Father Morini, who had founded the first priory of the Servites in America:

Dearly beloved friend and confrere,

In answer to your dear letter of the 19th of March, I can tell you that the Sisters of Viareggio are called Sisters of Mary of Sorrows. Like us, they have the Rule of St. Augustine. They have special constitutions based on the rule for our Third Order Secular with special clauses regarding school. They take simple vows that can be dispensed by the superior and director....They live by what they earn with the work of their own hands...because there are only a few who pay, and the poor pupils they keep gratis for the love of God and these come to more than 400.

Our Sisters retreated into a poor little house which they rented the 31st of October, 1852, when they were only four poor girls. Now, thanks be to God, they number 17, and they can live modestly well. I have ceased to be preoccupied about them....

Fr. Anthony M. Pucci, O.S.M.

The work which Father Pucci reserved to the Sisters, besides the school, was to teach catechism to the children, to give spiritual and material assistance to the women and girls of the parish.

In 1882, Father Anthony instituted the well-known Congregation of Christian Mothers, another proof of his apostolic zeal.

* * *

Anthony's work in restoring the physical and mental health of children began with the first Seaside Resort for Children in Italy.

In 1853 an association called Seaside Hospices, "Ospizi Marini," brought groups of sick children to the seashore during the summer months. Cholera swept over Tuscany in 1854 and 1855. As a result, the first children to take part in the program were sent to Viareggio in 1856. There were only three of them. By the summer of 1875, the children sent to the seaside numbered 1,044. Artists, writers, sculptors, and musicians were involved in initiating this work. Within a few years, there was a large building on the sands of Viareggio able to care for 400 to 500. It was, humorously enough, called the Palace of the Muses, thanks to the good financial help attained by gifts of art which artists offered to raise money for the seaside hospice. But the man whom Divine Providence inspired to sustain this noble work for about thirty years was Professor Joseph Barellai, a doctor in the flourishing hospital of Santa Maria Nuova. He cajoled his closest friends to help. Among them was the architect Casamorata, the first secretary of the "Ospizi Marini" and then president up to his death in 1879. When Doctor Barellai died in 1884, there were nineteen seaside resorts for children along the Adriatic and Mediterranean coasts of Italy.

The Order of the Servants of Mary is intimately bound up in the story of the first seaside resort for children of Italy and Europe. When the organizers of this work began, there arose a very serious problem - to whom should they entrust the sick children? Statistics of this time indicate that twenty percent of the population died between five and ten years of age. The greater part of these died from scrofula (a tuberculosis condition which causes enlargement and degeneration of the lymphatic glands). Who would take the responsibility of these children? We must remember that these children were chosen from among the more advanced cases of the disease. This was a first experiment. The responsibility was enormous. Dr. Barellai's parish church was the Church of the Annunziata in Florence. The doctor was right at home among religious. They encouraged him in his project, and finally gave their heart and soul to its realization. Father Provincial assumed the responsibility of locating a place and consulted Father Pucci of Viareggio. The Sisters were given charge of the children.

* * *

The infirmarian of the monastery at Florence, Brother Joseph Remaggi, accompanied the children to Viareggio. He went about begging alms for them so that the religious could finance the work. Each summer for eleven years the Sisters took care of the children in their convent. The Servites took care of the whole affair until 1876 when the Sisters, who had so much work elsewhere, were substituted by Sisters of Charity, and a civil administrator took charge. But the institution had already overcome its period of experimentation, and the seaside resort was already a fact in Italy. Father Anthony Pucci and Sister Juliana Lenci are the two figures who stand out eminently in this experiment of charity toward children.

Sister Juliana Lenci, the superior; organized the material details of the "colony." In these first years enormous sacrifices had to be made. The patients had to have special food. Sister Juliana's memories of these first trying years could be summed up in the words "fatigue and hunger."

Here is a letter that Father Provincial Mondini from Florence wrote to Anthony. It puts a documentary stamp on the great responsibility that Father Pucci had.

June 26, 1860 - Florence

Esteemed Father Prior;

Yesterday morning Doctor Barellai advised me that 30 children for the Seaside Camp will arrive there on the third or fourth of next month at the very latest. Please be so good as to tell the Directress (Sister Juliana Lenci) so that everything will be ready.

I believe that Doctor Barellai himself has notified the Directress that different fathers of the boys and girls had complained of the fact that last year some of the children had been made to wash dishes, sweep, etc. This year we would do better to abstain from making the little vacationers work in this way.

* * *

Concluding this brief sketch of the various charitable works of Father Pucci, we cannot but place him among the more active and intelligent organizers of the parish of today. He was incredibly far ahead of the times in the formation of the apostolate of the laity as we know it today.

Right now, the Roman Catholic Church is in need of a model for pastors who shepherd the sheep in each parish and to bring stray sheep back to the fold. The Little Pastor of

Viareggio, Anthony Pucci, who was declared a Saint on December 9,1962 in vibrant tones by Pope John XXIII, could be that model for all parish priests. His feast day is celebrated on January 12.

XV. VIATICUM

Viaticum is the Latin for "with you on the way." Father Anthony was with his parishioners all during the course of his pastoral work. He was with them on their way to their ultimate goal, Heaven. In this book we have tried to narrate his tireless activity. We have shown that, while he was young and vigorous, his body did not seem to resent its treatment of long, arduous work and prayer. But as the years began to pile up, we learn that Father Pucci was no longer physically strong.

In 1873, he wrote this short letter to his provincial: "I beg of you to send me a young Father to help me so that he can be prepared to take over the pastorate because I won't be able to carry out this work much longer. It is very important that we have a good pastor for the future."

We know from other documents how the Little Pastor resented the signs of old age. He noticed himself becoming tired much more readily. Father Alphonse Bozzi throws some light on this. "He dedicated himself so much to the ministry that he gave himself to work day and night. He had such a spirit of sacrifice that sometimes he came to the refectory so fatigued that he had to take a glass with both hands to lift it to his mouth."

* * *

A violent attack of bronchitis endangered the Little Pastor's life in 1890. The news spread like fire, "Father Anthony is sick." The parishioners gathered around their venerable father. Private and public triduums of prayer were offered for him. The suffering priest kept his habitual calm. He received the Sacraments of Extreme Unction and

Viaticum (Christ with him on the way to Heaven) and awaited death with these sentiments: "Here I am Lord. I abandon myself to You, hoping to rest soon in You."

These sacramental comforts gave Father Anthony new life. His congregation had prayed and God had listened to them. The doctors did their work and the priest was soon better. This was not his final hour. Soon he was back at his apostolate. Any other pastor might have tendered his resignation. Instead Father Anthony asked for two assistant pastors and went about his work for two more years.

It was already the vigil of his golden jubilee. The whole parish was secretly preparing to solemnly celebrate his fifty years as a priest. People from generation to generation loved and revered this holy friar. It delighted some of them to hear him say: "I knew your grandfather. He came here as a lad to learn his catechism, just like you. Ah, yes! I baptized your father; just as I baptized you!"

* * *

On a cold winter day in January, 1892, Father Pucci went on a sick call. He should have worn his wool mantle, but he had just made a present of it to an old man on the street. He shivered as he ministered to the sick man. Several times that day he returned to see how the patient was getting on. He trembled more each time from the cold but let no one know how he felt. He was not in the habit of revealing his own sufferings. Soon after he returned to his monastery he began to feel very ill. However, he continued to frequent the common acts - prayers, meals, spiritual exercises, Divine Office.

Great feasts like Epiphany in the Church begin the eve before, with the chanting of first vespers of the Divine

Office. As was his custom, Father Anthony presided at these beautiful services. During the chanting of the psalms, one of the enormous choir books slid off its stand and accidentally fell on him. Somehow it seemed prophetic.

On the Feast of the Three Kings, or Epiphany, he solemnly celebrated the Mass as pastor. Suddenly he began to cough, his complexion became red with fever, and large beads of sweat poured from his forehead. Desperately ill though he was, Father Anthony tranquilly continued celebrating Mass, absorbed in the Holy Sacrifice. But the ministers of the Mass noticed that every so often he shook convulsively with the cold. This he was unable to hide.

The Mass finished, his assistants gathered around him in the sacristy and slowly accompanied him to his room. Gently but firmly they convinced him that he should remain in bed. By now his temperature had risen and he trembled. Yet, he smiled to let his brethren know he was grateful for their kindness and that he acquiesced to this sickness in acceptance of God's will.

They called Dr. Triglia, who acted as the physician to the Servite community. He came immediately. Curiously enough, this was the same doctor who some years before had acted as an official physician to establish the miraculous cure of Anna Barsotti through the intercession of the Seven Holy Founders of the Servite Order.

After Dr. Triglia examined Father Pucci, he diagnosed his sickness as double pneumonia. The violent fever that he experienced soon rendered him unconscious for long periods and he was often delirious. His murmurings during these moments showed that his thoughts continued to center on his priestly pastoral role. He was the good pastor leading the sheep to the fold of the Master.

* * *

On the first day of his violent sickness, Father Anthony got out of bed at one o'clock in the morning, dressed himself, took his lantern, went out into the corridor and began to go downstairs. The lay brother on duty heard him. "Where are you going, Father, at this late hour?" he asked.

"Don't you know," said the Little Pastor, "that the Bishop is in church and there is nobody there to assist him?"

Another time he did the same thing. When asked where he was going, he answered: "I'm going to the church to give Communion."

* * *

After he got too weak to move Father Anthony carried out his apostolate right in bed. One moment he was confessing, another preaching, giving Communion, teaching catechism to the children, counseling them and warning them to pray fervently. In his delirium he returned subconsciously to all the things he loved during his life.

"When the serious sickness of Father Anthony was announced, the whole populace of Viareggio was filled with consternation. A few taps on the tower bell were all that was needed to bring people to the church praying for his cure. They crowded the priory seeking news," said Father Vincent Marraccini. They waited with sadness and preoccupation. There was a continuous stream at the priory door asking every hour how he was getting along.

"Always worse," the Brother would tell them. "I'm afraid now he is finished. There doesn't seem to be any remedy. The only thing that can save him now is a miracle. Pray for him."

Among those who came was the City Clerk, Mr. G. Del Beccaro. He was a Mason and, while he made no secret of his anti-clericalism, he was an intimate friend of Father Pucci. He knew, city official that he was, how much good Father Anthony had done for the people of Viareggio. He entered the room of the dying priest and when he saw the face of his friend, he cried like a child. (We have an eyewitness of this, Father Marraccini.)

* * *

The hours of his last agony were, for Father Pucci, conscious and unconscious, hours of prayer. His lips were moving constantly. In a lucid moment, one of the Fathers brought him *Viaticum*. The whole community of Fathers and Brothers was present. In a religious community, the superior has the right and the obligation to administer Holy Viaticum and the Sacrament of Extreme Unction (now called the Anointing of the Sick). Since it was the superior who was dying, his first assistant, or Vicar; carried out this duty. The devoted community tendered all the loving care they could to their beloved superior. The infirmarian cared for him at every moment. His confessor assisted him with great charity. The Mass for the Sick was celebrated and the general absolution was given.

* * *

On his part, Father Anthony received the last rites of the Church with great gratitude. He wanted to be with Christ now. To those who came to visit him in these last hours, his most frequent recommendation was, "Don't ever forget Our Lady of Sorrows."

He called aside a friend of the parish who had assisted him and asked him to bring food and clothing to some poor families. He called other intimate friends and spoke to them in the same way. Meanwhile, his room filled with a pleasant perfume. No one discovered from whence it originated. It is said this fragrance pervaded around the saint even during his wake in the church, up to the time he was laid to rest in the chapel of the cemetery.

A few hours before his death the Little Pastor lost consciousness. Meanwhile, all present recited the prayers of the dying. Just seconds after they finished, Father Pucci laid his head slightly to the right and expired.

The assistant pastor of St. Andrew's entered the following notice of death in the official book of the priory: "The 12th of January, 1892, Father Anthony, son of Augustine Pucci, pastor of St. Andrew, died at the age of 73 years - at two o'clock in the afternoon, fortified with all the Holy Sacraments and assisted by the priests. His body was transferred from the house to the church and then to the cemetery of this city (Viareggio) the evening of January 13th. Fra Stanislaus Borghini, Assistant Pastor."

They began immediately preparing the body and clothed it decently. The persons who were assigned to this loving office declared that not only did the body exude no odor of decomposition but that "it seemed to give forth a special fragrance that all attributed to supernatural causes."

No sooner had the holy body been clothed in the monastic habit than the bell was tolled, announcing to the people of Viareggio the sad news of the death of their Little

Pastor. He was brought down to the front parlor of the priory. An enormous crowd converged at the doors to get a last glimpse of their beloved pastor. The crowds gradually increased to the point where the city had to send a number of policemen to maintain order. It was an unforgettable sight. There was hardly anyone who could restrain his tears.

"A saint is dead...!"
"The father of the poor is dead!"
"He did so much good for me!"
Tributes like these abounded.

Ulysses Michetti witnessed the sad scene. He recounts that little pieces of the priest's habit and his personal effects were snatched as relics of their pastor whom they already revered as a saint. "I myself," he said, "had to cut several hundred little pieces with a pair of scissors and even these were not enough for all. I had to go in search of other personal clothing of the servant of God to the point that I believe there is none of the personal clothing of the Little Pastor left."

The long lines of pilgrims continued until far into the night. They came from Viareggio and from all the countryside about. All came to pay their last respects to this giant of a priest, this Little Pastor they loved.

* * *

In death, Father Anthony was placed upon his bier dressed in a new habit. His head was crowned with a biretta signifying that he was a master of theology. He had asked for a simple, wooden coffin, no flowers, and one candle to symbolize his faith. Instead, his funeral was triumphant. The City Council, though made up in great part by Masons, decreed civic honors for him and paid all the funeral expenses. The Confraternity of Mercy placed its most luxurious hearse at the disposition of the church. Stores and schools were closed as a mark of respect. Contemporaries note that the whole population walked behind the hearse. No one had ever seen such a grand spectacle. Thousands of people walked in the cold rain that afternoon of January 13, 1892.

It was night when the cortege arrived at the new cemetery and two hundred torches gave it a mystical solemnity as though their bearers were accompanying precious relics. The crowds asked that the coffin be opened again. By order of the City Council he was buried in the cemetery chapel, even though the Little Pastor had desired to be buried in the ground with his parishioners.

Because his remains were buried in the chapel of the new cemetery, they were required by law to be encased in a zinc coffin. A marble stone was placed over the tomb with the inscription: "To Father Anthony Pucci - The City Council and the People of Viareggio - Q.M.P. - 1892."

The Committee named to carry out the obsequies of the Little Pastor invited the noted sculptor Di Ciolo to take an impression of the features of our saint and to sculpture a monument over the tomb. A likeness was enthroned in the wall of the chapel in the center of the church, inscribed "The people of Viareggio - to Father Anthony Pucci."

On the occasion of the funeral, Father Raphael Sarri, O.S.M., published an "In Memoriam" the day after Anthony Pucci's death. This synthesized the life of Father Pucci and made him loved again in the hearts of those who knew him. Thousands of copies quickly disappeared, and numerous outsiders held this as a precious souvenir. Many more thousands could not obtain a copy!

The papers in the whole region were filled with accounts of the funeral. One example, the *Corriere Toscano,* on January 18, 1892 printed the following: "... it was my good fortune to be present at one of these manifestations, which were as moving as they were impressive; and I confess with all sincerity that I have never seen anything like it in my life. I am speaking of a poor, little member of the Order of Servants of Mary, who was a type of humility and modesty incarnate. He took great care to hide from men's eyes his outstanding virtues, chief of which was his Christian charity, a noble, generous and prudent charity....

"You could say that the whole city took part in the cortege, which resulted in such an imposing and moving affair....Moving about in the crowds, I heard everywhere words of benediction to the memory of the beloved pastor.

"Few have gone to rest in the midst of general sorrow as did the Little Pastor of Viareggio...because few have known how to merit, as he did, universal sorrow.

* * *

During his lifetime Father Anthony was revered as a saint. In the liturgy of the Mass of the Dead there is an oft repeated theme from Psalm 111: "The just shall be in everlasting remembrance." Father Pucci was a just man, witnesses Ulysses Michette: "He was considered a saint by all classes of persons, the ordinary people, the learned, lay people, clergy, religious, and even his enemies; and this opinion was the fruit of his virtues, especially charity".

Others added, "The fame of his sanctity was not restricted to Viareggio, but the Fathers of our Order held him in esteem, and others as well considered him a saint." Father Ducceschi testified: "Among these I remember Bishop Batignani of Montepulciano, who told me, 'I, too, knew him and considered him a saint.'" The same sentiments were shared by Cardinal Galimberti, Apostolic Nuncio to Vienna, by Archbishop Nicholas Ghilardi of Lucca, and by Ferdinand Conte Capponi of Pisa.

Many families in Viareggio kept his picture on an altar with flowers and candles. Just as when he lived he was a refuge for every want, so after his death the people continued to resort to him. They did not ask in vain. Enthusiasm for Father Pucci mounted. Eight years after his death, in 1900, a committee of young Catholics on behalf of the citizens requested the City Council to name a street after him. That year the City Council was still predominantly anti-clerical. It gave a resounding 'No' to the plea. It answered, "Father Pucci was a priest and he did nothing more than was his duty." In turning down this simple honor for the Little Pastor; the Council unwittingly provided one of the greatest testimonials of his holiness. "He did nothing more than was his duty."

The lively desire of the people to dwell more and more upon his life and virtues was satisfied by memorial celebrations, sermons and other gatherings in his honor. Father Anthony's fame spread overseas. Bishop Chiarlo, Apostolic Nuncio of Brazil, preached more than once on the Little Pastor. In Chicago, in the late 1880's, his good friend Father Morini, founder of the American Province of Servites, often held him up for imitation to the people as well as to his fellow friars.

In 1907, the Catholic Youth of Viareggio, newly-vitalized by saintly directives from Rome, set up the Parochial Associations under the name of Father Anthony Pucci. The Associations blossomed marvelously and brought forth fruit.

Meanwhile the people of Viareggio kept insisting in their demands to honor their beloved Father Pucci. They wanted monuments to him. They wanted him brought back from the cemetery so as to be near to them. They wanted a street named for him.

The Young Catholic Circle wanted to be in the first ranks in their endeavor to honor the friend of youth, Father Anthony. It was instrumental in bringing about that monument to him sculptured by Di Ciolo. The fine likeness of the pastor of Viareggio was unveiled in his Church of St. Joseph on January 11, 1911. It had the admiration of the whole countryside. Large numbers of all these religious and civil associations around Viareggio participated. There were many discourses. The official orator was Most Reverend Charles Chiarlo, who recalled in his talk the wish of the people to bring the remains of the saintly pastor back to his Church of St. Andrew. The press, far and wide, amply covered the celebrations.

*　*　*

Confronted by such feelings of esteem toward Father Pucci, the City Council felt the time had come to name one of the public thoroughfares in his honor. What street did they choose? Certainly they did not want to give a member of a religious order a place of honor such as one of the spacious avenues along the sea. They preferred to assign him one of the old streets of the city called "Avenue of Repose."

Although not the highest tribute that the Viareggio City Council could have given, it was extraordinary for 1916 and helped to satisfy the longings of the people to have their pastor so remembered.

* * *

The day after Father Anthony's death Mayor E. Alexander Tomei met in emergency session with some members of the City Council concerning funeral arrangements. This action was subsequently ratified by a full meeting of the City Council which met on January 25. The text reads in part as follows:

The Province of Lucca, City of Viareggio, 1892. Extract from the Register of the Deliberations of the City Council, No. 283, extraordinary session, first meeting. Open to the Public.

Having read the letter of invitation from the Mayor, the honorable components of the Communal Council of Viareggio gathered in the community office of Viareggio at fifteen hours, 25th of January, 1892. Eighteen gentlemen were present (the names follow)....

There was a reading of the following deliberation taken by the assembly in their session of the 13th of the current month, with regard to the funeral arrangements to be given to Mr. Eustace Pucci, Pastor of St. Andrew in this city, who died the 12th day of this month.

The Mayor brought to the attention of the assembly that the Servite Don Eustace Pucci, who was about 47 years pastor of the Church of St. Andrew in this city, died yesterday.

Let it be known that, apart from his character as a Catholic priest, Father Pucci as a man was worthy of praise from the city insofar as his life was a continual and indefatigable apostolate for humanity...; that he merited praise and encomium when, still a young man in the years 1854, 1855 and 1856 he served with exemplary zeal the victims of deathly cholera; that he was always there wherever there was sorrow to be assuaged, decisions to be made, always an example of true virtue.

That he, never concerning himself with politics, leaving this to those whose job it is, gave an example of how a cleric should conduct himself in civil affairs.

That he aroused general esteem and benevolence and that the Council, interpreting the sentiments of the population, ought to give to this man who merits it a special honor in his burial and to this effect he, the Mayor, proposes that the remains of Father Pucci be buried in the church of the new cemetery.

Moreover, he requests Knight Alexander Raffaelli, President of the committee set up for the funeral of the honorable deceased, to engage a band for the funeral procession...the Musical Corps G. Pacini.

The Council voted sixteen to two in favor of all of the Mayor's requests.

This document alone would suffice to show how much the Little Pastor was mourned. On the surface, the Council evidenced a cool etiquette. Nonetheless it could not hide the Christian sentiments that filled the hearts of the councilors at the death of the saint. We note the various ways the saint is referred to in the document. First, he is referred to as "Mr. Eustace Pucci," then he becomes "the Servite Don Eustace

Pucci," then further on, prescinding from his "character as a Catholic priest" he becomes "Father Pucci." As a finale to this metamorphosis, look at the epitaph inscribed on the tomb of the saint, likewise approved by the Council: "To Father Anthony Pucci - the Council and the People of Viareggio."

* * *

God is admirable in His saints. Each of us has His image. But the saints are His masterpieces. During their lives they suffer like marble under the hand of the sculptor.

God does not cease to be admirable in His saints after they are dead. A new phase begins. God inspires devotees with confidence in the saints as their patrons. They obtain favors and miracles from Him. God permits His saints to approach Him for favors, though obviously He could grant these quite as well Himself. And what favors must He grant for a Servant of His Mother, such as St. Anthony Mary Pucci!

The Church, in turn, gathers these manifestations of holiness, sifts them, tests them, dismisses or approves them, in what is known as the process of canonization.

* * *

St. Anthony Pucci rested in the cemetery chapel where the Council had consigned him, until April 18, 1920. That day the whole populace rejoiced in accompanying him back to the Church of St. Andrew in Viareggio. The imposing cortege was the biggest in the city's history since the Little Pastor's own funeral back in 1892. It rained on the day of his funeral. It rained this day, too. Present in the procession was the celebrated Giacomo Puccini. More significant still was the cure of a child. We will let his mother tell the story.

"I remember," says Paolina Matraia, "that on the occasion of the transfer of the body of Father Pucci from the cemetery to the Church of St. Andrew, my son wanted to come. I would not have permitted him to come because it was raining and he was suffering from a head injury with seven stitches. He did take part in the procession, though, and was drenched, all the time confident that Father Pucci would cure him more quickly. In fact, when the body was brought into the church and the coffin opened, he kissed the relics and touched his head to them with faith. The next day when he went for treatment the doctor removed the bandages, verified the cure, and sent him home."

The first marvelous cure used for the beatification of Anthony happened in 1929. Olga Bruni di Silvo, seventeen years of age, lived in Massa, Italy. The gravity of her sickness was attested by Dr. Nicholas Zonder and other doctors whom he consulted in making the diagnosis of tubercular meningitis. The relatives, perceiving that there was no hope, had recourse to God Almighty, invoking the intercession of Father Anthony Pucci. It was Canon Formai who was called to administer the last sacraments to the girl. He placed a relic of Anthony under her pillow and encouraged them to pray to him. After some hours of praying, her condition improved, as was witnessed by Dr. Zonder, and she was completely cured. Dr. Zonder had declared, before the prayers to St. Anthony, that, "if a cure should happen it would be truly miraculous and supernatural and would be completely outside the natural order. As far as medical science has observed, not only according to my observations but also those of three illustrious doctors who saw the patient in consultation with me, the prognosis is absolutely hopeless." The cure was acclaimed by all as a miracle.

* * *

Mary Zappelli, born May 18, 1903, was the widow of Adolph Lippi. In the first days of December, 1934, she contracted scarlatina while assisting her son, Angelo, infected with the same disease. Her condition turned into hemorrhaging nephritis, according to her doctor, Rudolph Fini. Despite medication, her condition worsened, until she lapsed into coma. Two specialists, Dr. Tabarracci and Dr. Torn, confirmed the diagnosis. Mary Zappelli's condition was considered hopeless and she was dying. The night of the 22nd of December 1934, her relatives took a relic of the clothing of St. Anthony immersed it in water which they gave her to drink, invoking the help of the Servant of God. She went to sleep tranquilly.

Awaking at eight in the morning, now fully conscious, she felt well, asked for food, and drank a glass of milk. Dr. Fini examined her the same morning to find everything normal. She remained in bed for a few days as a matter of prudence, doing some sewing and knitting. Then she immediately took up her laborious family life. Her cure was recognized by those present, and by the doctor as instantaneous and miraculous.

* * *

God is marvelous in His saints. Even on the street named after Father Anthony - 62 Antonio Pucci Street - in Viareggio a miracle occurred. A young man at this address, Gregory Simonetti, worked as a mechanic in a shop called Baroni. On September 2,1937, he injured himself on a nail.

He went to the doctor that same evening. He diagnosed the illness as a fever deriving from his sweating out in the open air.

Two nights later Dr. Rudolf Fini answered an emergency sick call to discover this same lad suffering with evident symptoms of tetanus infection. He was ordered brought to the hospital.

Notwithstanding the anti-tetanus treatment administered by the attendant physician, Dr. Paoletti, general septicemia developed with all the external signs and severe pain. The hospital authorities confessed their powerlessness in the case, already too far advanced. They called the priest, who administered the last rites of the Church.

The youth's mother, Clodovea, seeing no hope, asked that he be brought home to die. Dr. Fini came to assist the young man in his agony. He found the funeral arrangements already made and the boy's burial clothes laid out.

Meanwhile, a neighbor; Fulvio Puccetti, sent over a relic of St. Anthony Pucci and encouraged the mother to invoke him with confidence. She placed the relic on her son. The lad was too weak to join her; his death imminent, but she prayed. After some hours, her son awoke, moved about, and began to speak. In a few days his cure was complete.

* * *

God worked other miracles through St. Anthony Mary Pucci. Two of these were chosen for his canonization:

Carolina Pucci Cupisti of Viareggio, Italy, mother of a family, suffered from a dislocated right hip bone from birth. It made her limp on her left foot.

In August, 1938, she fell down aboard a boat belonging to her husband and she began to experience severe pain in the affected part.

She immediately consulted the doctor. X-rays showed deforming of the joints with congenital dislocation. For about six months, Carolina was confined to bed with a plaster cast. Various medicines could not however take away the pain which now spread to other parts of her body as well. In spite of countless treatments, she became worse and found it increasingly difficult to walk.

The pain became unbearable. The surgeon proposed to remove the source of the pain as a last resort. She, meanwhile, prayed to Blessed Anthony Mary Pucci. On April 25,1953, at the end of the prayers for the Rogation Days, she repeated her prayers at the tomb of Blessed Anthony, begging for strength to at least bear the operation with patience.

All at once her pain stopped. The woman arose from her place, laid down her crutch, began to walk about the church, went up to the Communion rail, knelt down normally and received Holy Communion. Returning home, she walked upstairs unaided much to the astonishment of those who knew her. All heralded it as a miracle.

Doctors, experts and the official medical group of the Sacred Congregation of Rites openly allowed that this cure was beyond the order of nature and its power.

* * *

A sixteen year old farmer Joseph Gomez (Jose Altidoro Barrietos Gomez) received the other miraculous cure from Blessed Anthony Pucci. Joseph was from the village of

Cohaique in the Apostolic Vicariate of Aysen in Chile, South America. On February 10, 1953, he was riding a heavily loaded ox-cart when he fell flat on the ground. The right wheel of the cart rolled over his abdomen and pelvis severely injuring him. His father and the man who owned the wagon brought him to the nearest hospital, arriving the evening of the same day. Two doctors attending him found him suffering from persistent vomiting with high fever, internal hemorrhage, signs of obstruction and severe pain. In brief, his condition was very grave.

Clinical examinations showed contusions in the abdomen and pelvic region affecting the internal organs with dangerous lesions. An X-ray taken some years afterwards showed that the ischial-pubic bone had also been fractured. With this unhappy prognosis by March 14, 1953, the doctors suspended treatment.

With hope of human aid gone, Blessed Anthony Mary Pucci was invoked in special prayers the evening of March 14,1953. The young farmer fell into a peaceful sleep. He awoke the morning of the 15th feeling completely cured. He arose, dressed and walked about unaided. The other patients of the hospital saw it at once as a miracle.

On the testimony of doctors, relatives, nurses and other witnesses this cure was declared miraculous, beyond the natural law, on July 7, 1962.

* * *

There are great men who became great at their own expense. They expended their God-given gifts for their fellowmen. Of such cloth are the saints woven. Such a man was our Father Anthony Pucci, O.S.M., whom Pope John

XXIII deigned to canonize "Saint Anthony, Pastor of Viareggio," on December 9,1962.

May we imitate this blessed man, so poor in spirit, who is now in the Kingdom of Heaven, as we pray fervently, "Saint Anthony Pucci, Servant of Mary, Pastor of Viareggio, Shepherd of Souls, pray for us now and at the hour of our death. Amen."

CONCLUSION

Saint Anthony Pucci's remains lie beneath the altar in the parish church. He is clothed in the Servite habit of his Order; with stole and surplice to signify his priestly office. The body, in a good state of preservation, is in a glass coffin. A silver mask covers the head. The altar is beautiful, but a really worthy shrine awaits the generosity of some grateful client.

Part of his body was transferred to the Servite Generalate of San Marcello in Rome, Italy. The author venerated it often during his six years of residence at this exquisitely beautiful church, one of the most ancient and venerable titular churches of Rome.

Devotion to Saint Anthony Pucci, the Pastor of Viareggio, has grown wherever there are pastors and parishioners all over the Christian world, especially in Servite churches in Africa, Australia, Canada, Europe, Mexico, South America, and the United States of America.

Finito di stammmpare nel mese
di ottobre 1985
dalla tipografia Citta Nuova della P.A.M.O.M.
Largo Cristina di Svezia, 17
00165 Roma tel. 5813475/82